T0078263

Navigating the
SHADOWLANDS

A True Story of Survival, Deliverance, and Transformation

DAVID ALLAN JACQUES

A Memoir

Scripture quotations taken from the New American Standard Bible®, Copyright © 1960, 1962, 1963, 1968, 1971, 1972, 1973, 1975, 1977, 1995 by The Lockman Foundation. Used by permission. (www.Lockman.org)

Archway Publishing books may be ordered through booksellers or by contacting:

Archway Publishing
1663 Liberty Drive
Bloomington, IN 47403
www.archwaypublishing.com
1 (888) 242-5904

Because of the dynamic nature of the Internet, any web addresses or links contained in this book may have changed since publication and may no longer be valid. The views expressed in this work are solely those of the author and do not necessarily reflect the views of the publisher, and the publisher hereby disclaims any responsibility for them.

Any people depicted in stock imagery provided by Thinkstock are models, and such images are being used for illustrative purposes only. Certain stock imagery © Thinkstock.

ISBN: 978-1-4808-3751-5 (sc)
ISBN: 978-1-4808-3752-2 (e)

Library of Congress Control Number: 2016915686

Print information available on the last page.

Archway Publishing rev. date: 05/03/2017

"The Lord is my shepherd. I shall not want. He maketh me lie down in green pastures; He leadeth me beside the still waters. He restoreth my soul; He leadeth me in paths of righteousness for His name's sake. Yea, though I walk through the valley of the shadow of death, I fear no evil: for Thou art with me; Thy rod and Thy staff they comfort me. Thou preparest a table before me in the presence of mine enemies; Thou anointest my head with oil; my cup runneth over. Surely goodness and mercy will follow me all the days of my life, and I will dwell in the house of the Lord forever."
PSALM 23 *KJV*

CONTENTS

PART III   A Journey of Transformation

ACKNOWLEDGEMENTS

I WOULD LIKE TO ACKNOWLEDGE the following people for their contributions to my life and to this story. I will be forever grateful for those who helped shape me into the man I am today. As time goes on, it becomes more obvious to me that we are all different tools in the hand of God that He uses to carve, shape, mold, and even break us at times so that we might receive His salvation, deliverance, healing and freedom.

The hero in this story is my God and Savior Jesus Christ for His sovereign intervention in my life. He was the One healing, delivering, redeeming and restoring me. Without Him there would be no story, and the outcome of my life would have had a much darker ending.

I want to thank God for my amazing wife Lori and for her love, patience, and understanding. She is an incredible gift that God continually uses to "sand" my rough edges. I am clearly a better man because of her. She has not only been a sounding board for me, but has taken time to review my work. Her honest appraisal helped make this book possible.

I want to thank my mom and dad for their love, support, and years of sacrifice. Thank you for all that you invested in my life. Thank you for your willingness to be vulnerable and allowing me to share part of your story as well as mine.

I want to thank my Marine Corps brothers John Curtis, Robert Domecq, and Tim Jones for their strength and for sharing their steadfast faith and friendship with me during a very challenging period in my life.

I want to thank my lifelong friends Steve Hampton, Arthur Andrews, Tim Gray, Steve Burger, Todd Foerch, Derek Morita, Karen Schooner, Lisa Doty (Gray) and J-Michael Wuestemann for being family to me when I needed it most. Thank you all for speaking into my life, for praying for me, and for loving me. You were all channels of God's healing and grace. I am forever in your debt, and I love you all.

A special thanks to my designated readers: Teresa Giovati Archer (my editor and friend), Karen Clatterbuck (my mother-in-law), Lori Jacques (my wife), and Doug Jacques (my dad). Thank you for your honesty, analysis and constructive insight. Your insight and counsel made this a better book, and your contributions were invaluable.

Lastly, I want to acknowledge two of our fathers in the faith, the late Pastor Chuck Smith of Calvary Chapel, Costa Mesa, and the late John Wimber of Anaheim Vineyard Christian Fellowship. Indirectly, these two men greatly influenced my life, and had a far reaching impact on the lives of so many. We honor you and your legacy of faith.

A WORD FROM THE AUTHOR

THE STORY I AM ABOUT to share with you is all true. Some of the details may have some inaccuracies because of the lapse of time and my own limited memory. Also, I have modified some parts of the story to protect the privacy of those involved. For that reason, I have changed some of the names and places involved. That said, what I share with you is my incredible journey through this life and my account of what I have come to know as *navigating the shadowlands.*

BACKWARD AND FORWARD

1987

IMAGINE HAVING EVERYTHING THAT EVER mattered to you suddenly ripped away overnight. Imagine having everything you could ever want and then losing it all. If you have any understanding of that experience, any inkling at all, then you will appreciate my story and the miracle that transpired in my life.

It took me two weeks to process out of the military. I received my honorable discharge on November 14,[th] 1987. After my discharge I moved back into my mother's house in Orange County. I was an emotional wreck and I knew it. I had just lost my closest loved one and any career options I formerly had. I was mentally and emotionally on the brink of my sanity. My life was completely destroyed. I had somehow sabotaged everything that I held most precious to me. My heart was broken. I was in despair, and I had this black cloud hanging over me. Anxiety plagued me, and I lived with a constant sense of impending doom, feeling like the other shoe was about to drop at any moment. I was surviving. I was existing and God seemed a million miles away.

Rage was seething underneath my hurting exterior. I hated myself for what I had allowed myself to become. I was lost and in severe pain. There seemed to be no answers and no options.

It was late November in 1987; I pulled into a parking lot, found a spot under a shade tree, and parked my car. My face contorted, and I broke down and cried against the steering wheel. The pain was deep and excruciating. Now there was no distraction, the pain and despair seemed all-consuming. My crying soon became sobbing, and then my sobbing became wailing. I gathered up a towel, and held it over my mouth to muffle the sound. The pain was deep and raw. My nose began to run. The flood gates were open and there was no stopping it.

As twilight came, I was tormented by self-condemnation: *I've failed at everything I've ever tried. I'm sick, very sick. There is really nothing left for me here, and this pain in my soul is unbearable. I can't take this anymore...I could end it though...I could end it all right now. Why not?*

I cried on and off for hours. That night went on forever. I was still being torn up inside. As the sun went down and darkness closed in, the pain became even more excruciating. I cried out to God, begging Him to take away the pain. I began to seriously contemplate suicide, anything to escape the depth of agony and the overwhelming sense of loss I was experiencing at that moment. *How would I kill myself? How would I really do it?* My mind drifted as I thought about the people who cared about me...*Who really cares about me?* The gravity of my future tormented me as thoughts of my failure projected visions of me being homeless and walking the streets destitute.

2015

My name is David Allan Jacques, and I am a walking miracle. Today by the grace of God, I am happily married to a beautiful woman. I have two wonderful kids now in college. Moreover, I am blessed to have my own home. I work as a member of the security staff for the various county facilities in our town. Lately, I've been assigned to one of the psychological health facilities. I monitor the building to keep everyone safe, as some of the clientele can get "excited" from time to time. Every day I see a wide spectrum of dysfunction represented in the people who darken the door of this facility.

As I observe the amalgamation of humanity that comes through these doors, it's always amusing to notice the various unique and even strange idiosyncrasies and tics displayed in people.

- A fortyish year old man walks in stiffly, like a penguin teetering from side to side. His mouth moves continually with no audible sound coming out.
- A young homeless man comes in white as a ghost, his eyes painted dark with mascara.
- A woman in her mid-thirties walks in hirky-jerky, loud and boisterous, using demonstrative hand motions. She's oblivious to her own volume as she greets those standing right in front of her. Having no filter for what's appropriate, she speaks whatever comes to her mind as people around her grimace.
- A woman comes in struggling with anxiety, unable to sit still; she cries out desperately begging the staff to be medicated.
- Two men are escorted in by a case manager walking very slowly with their arms hanging down to their sides, staring out, looking shell-shocked, needing guidance, looking lost, like fifty-year-old children in need of a mother.

As I observe this odd stream of humanity, I'm reminded that I could have easily ended up in a similar condition had God not intervened and literally crashed into my life so many years ago. Had it not been for a miraculous and divine touch of God on my life, I would most certainly be homeless, in jail, or *dead*.

That said, the story I am about to share with you is so unbelievable and fantastic that I feel compelled to share it.

This is my story...

PART I

A Journey of Survival

CHAPTER 1

Welcome to the Jungle

SEVERAL HARD BLOWS TO THE face, then I was pushed to the ground. I was six years old, in tears and complete shock. It was my first fight ever on the primary school playground of Excelsior Elementary after our move to the new neighborhood. The other kid was a year older and a lot bigger. I had never been in a fight before. I didn't even know how to fight. So there I sat on the ground paralyzed by fear until the other kid finally walked away. It would be my first lesson in "the law of the jungle."

Of course, it didn't end there. It never does. Perceived weakness only encourages more oppression and greater persecution on the part of your enemies. It's a fundamental principle, even in international politics. To maintain peace in the world you need to have a bigger stick than the next guy; for countries, that might mean having a bigger army or a bigger bomb than your neighboring nation. I knew nothing of such things as a six-year-old child. I was never warned that this might happen. I was never taught how to defend myself. The other kids heckled me mercilessly. Feelings of vulnerability washed over me. I felt like an alien in a foreign land. None of that mattered though, because from that day forward, it was as though I had a big target painted on my chest.

I did the only thing that I thought I could do. I went to my teacher and told her the whole story. Funny, she didn't seem at all interested in the details of my altercation. She simply sent us both to the principal's office. The school's principal, Mr. Morris, listened to both sides patiently before calling our parents to have us both picked up for the day. I was home an hour later. I remember my mom being sympathetic and upset. My dad got home that evening, and after he was told, he threw a fit. My dad had an explosive temper, and I feared his anger. I think he was mad that I would have to miss a day of school. Nonetheless, the problem remained unresolved, and I received no instruction as to how to handle it. I suppose my parents both thought it was an anomaly, something that rarely happens, and that there was nothing to worry about. After all, boys will be boys, right?

This was my introduction to the new school. My parents, my two younger sisters, and I had lived in North Hollywood before the move. As a five year old boy, I resembled a bleached blond stick figure as I ran around our street. I was always curious, active, inquisitive, and possessed a boundless imagination. Typically, I had difficulty staying still for any length of time, and I annoyed my sisters constantly. Most of the kids in my neighborhood were older. Because I was younger and smaller, I was always excluded from the make-believe army wars the boys would have in the vacant dirt lot near our house. I often watched while a kid named Lance would dig his fox hole with an Etool and build his fort. The fort was usually made of cardboard boxes, old plywood and assorted other debris. Then I would help Lance collect his arsenal of dirt clod bombs. Once both parties were ready, the war would begin. The objective was to knock down the other kid's fort using only dirt clods. The kid with the last fort standing would be declared the victor. The war would usually last until ones fort was razed or somebody got hit in the head with a dirt clod. It was all in good fun.

A year later we moved to Garden Grove into an L-shaped, three bedroom, tract-home with a pool. This house was at the end of a cul-de-sac, and this is where my life would radically change. The area seemed nice at the time, but the neighborhood was a little rougher than I was used to. I was still of a tender age, naive, and had never been taught how to fight. In fact, it never occurred to me that I would even need to know how to fight. This is what must have made me an easy and obvious target to any predators on the playground, so it didn't take long for trouble to start. I must have looked vulnerable because I soon became a bully magnet. I was experiencing real fear for the first time. The kids were brutal and unmerciful. I didn't dare fight back, fearing even greater wrath and more pain, but my inaction and passivity only made things worse. The threats soon became commonplace and anxiety plagued me as I watched the clock, dreading break times and lunches.

The bullying continued off and on throughout elementary school. I was reluctant to discuss it with my dad fearing his reaction. My dad had a type-A personality, and was very autocratic and military in his parenting style. With high standards and expectations, it was very important to him that we did our best and performed well. My dad was also driven and performance-oriented. He loved sports and signed me up for baseball as soon as I was old enough to play. Dad was always family-centered and very private about his personal life as well as subjects relating to money, faith, and my late grandfather. It seemed he never liked to talk about his dad. This was a mystery to me for some time. Later, I learned that when my dad was eighteen, his dad (my grandfather) died in a construction accident. The loss was so traumatic and painful for my dad that he had unconsciously determined not to let anyone get close to him again. This would shape many of his future family relationships. He could be a loving parent, but he could also wall himself off from the family at times. Dad never liked to share on an emotional level and would avoid being vulnerable in any way. If he felt you were getting too close to a subject he deemed off-limits, he would push you away by saying, "It's none of your business!" We soon learned what subjects were safe, and avoided those that were forbidden.

In contrast, my mother was a socialite and a party girl, and she had a more casual approach to life. This later became-the rub in their marriage. Mom came from a family of nine and had six siblings: two sisters and four brothers. Her mother, Grammy as we called her, came from a well-to-do family and was a woman of some means. She already owned a large house when she married my grandfather, whom we called Grampy.

Grampy liked to drink and began to consume the family's resources after children came along. Grammy worked full-time to provide for my mother and her six siblings. Needless to say, a single income didn't go very far toward feeding seven children. Grampy continued to drink most of the family's money away. Grammy loved him and believed in staying committed through thick and thin. Over time, she had to make adjustments to meet the family's increasing financial needs. One of these adjustments involved downsizing the house they were living in. Grampy was never free from alcohol. It was very hard on Grammy and the children. Eventually they ended up in a hovel since Grampy had continued to drink away much of the family's income. Those hard times no doubt had an impact on my mother and her siblings.

Consequently, my mother eventually turned to alcohol as well. Mother was fun-loving, and life was all about celebration and relationships. Being virtual opposites, mom's and dad's two very different approaches to life became a source of contention in their relationship.

In the fourth grade I was nine years old when my dad, moving up in his company, was experiencing more pressure and demands on him both at work and at home. Alcohol was often present in our house and fueled much of the conflict between my parents. The chaos and instability at home naturally created a lot of anxiety in me and my siblings as we began to anticipate our parent's separation. My imagination would run wild as I began to ponder the question, *What's going to happen to us if Dad leaves?* This fear made it difficult to focus on schoolwork which, in turn, had a direct impact on my grades. To compound matters, I was still experiencing threats at school.

In the fifth grade things started to escalate. One day I was walking home from school. The route was a half-mile, not long, but not short either. I came to the end of the school playground fence where the housing started. At the end there was a house with a yard that had several tall evergreens. I could see a group of kids standing around in the yard for no apparent reason. I could feel their eyes and all their attention on me. They had been anticipating an event and had come to watch. As I made my approach, three boys suddenly came out from behind the trees. They had been waiting for me. I immediately recognized the leader, a tough, aggressive kid named Johnny Stogel. I knew then that it was going to be a bad day. Johnny and his friends quickly proceeded to jump me. I received a flurry of blows to the face. Fearing something worse might happen if I tried to fight back, I sat there and took it. The fear paralyzed me. I tried to shield myself, covering my face with my arms trying to survive the episode. Finally bored, they walked away. However, my passivity only encouraged them for the rest of the school year, and I began to get beaten on a regular basis.

One day after a particularly copious beating, I came home in tears. My mom was in the kitchen cleaning, and when she saw me she was visibly upset. Once she looked me over and saw that nothing was broken, she said, "Go tell your dad what happened." I think she thought that my dad was going to do something about it. I went into the bedroom, still crying, and before I could get a word out, my dad blew up! "Get out of here, you crybaby!" To his credit, my dad didn't want me playing the victim, and he was just trying to help me toughen up a bit. However, I left the house feeling very rejected and alone, my fear now increasing.

I realized that I was on my own with no protection. So, I began thinking...

I did a lot of thinking. It was a survival mechanism. Creating distraction by retreating into my head enabled me to cope. I loved to think, dream, invent, imagine and analyze things. This, however, led to a lot of trouble in class as I escaped on these mental trips. (See the movie, "The Secret Life of Walter Mitty." That character was a lot like me as a kid). The teacher was always calling on me at the most inopportune times. On numerous occasions I was jolted out of my fantasyland and sucked back into reality only to see the teacher standing before me, tapping her foot, waiting for an answer to a question I didn't know. This got me labeled "the daydreamer" by the faculty and "space cadet" by my peers.

To avoid reprimand and ridicule, I tried to think of more constructive ways of escaping my troubles. I dreamt about running away. I thought that someday I would hike for miles out into the woods and build my own cabin. I could camp, fish, and live off the land. Then I would be safe, secluded, and far away from all my troubles. This started me thinking about joining the Boy Scouts. I asked my parents if I could join. My parents were supportive and signed me up after my tenth birthday. I started attending Scout meetings once a week in the evening at my elementary school. At these meetings I noticed immediately that some of the older Scout members were acting aloof and adversarial toward me. A number of the boys shared a significant history together, and I wasn't part of any of their stories. Consequently, they ignored me or cut me out of their conversations. As usual, nepotism ruled the day as our Scoutmaster's son was very much in charge.

After several weeks, I was able to participate in my first camping trip. The trip was in the late fall and took us into California's San Bernardino Mountain range. When we arrived at our campsite it was late in the day, and there was a crisp bite in the mountain air as we unloaded the van. The smell of pine trees and burning wood were prominent. We all helped set up camp. Everybody pitched in, and it wasn't long before we had our camp organized and our tents set up in a semi-circle with a campfire in the middle. There was still a little daylight left, so the boys wanted to go for a short hike into the woods. Our Scoutmaster stayed behind to tend the camp. His son, a tall, lanky kid with dark hair and dark eyes, would be leading the hike.

It was nearing twilight. The increasing chill in the air prickled our skin, but we weren't going to be gone for long. Dappled sunlight gave a dim illumination through the forest canopy as we began our trek. The mood became strangely quiet as we hiked into the woods. After about a mile in, we came to a clearing amidst a number of trees. There was a stump in the middle of this clearing. That's when this little venture took a turn for the worst. The other Scouts seemed to know this place as though they had been there before. Maybe they had come here with other newbies. I soon became aware that there was an agenda. The older boys all started to insist that I go through their initiation ritual. They explained that they did this with all the new members. The boys told me that I couldn't be one of them if I didn't go through the initiation. The atmosphere took on a dark, threatening mood at that point. Our leader, the Scoutmaster's son, was an older boy, and there was something menacing about him. He told me that I was to put my hand down on the stump of the tree. Then the leader would swing a hatchet. I would be expected to pull my hand out of the way just before my fingers were cut off. "Are you going to be brave enough?" He asked, "Or are you going to wimp out?"

At first I wasn't sure if they were kidding with me, but there was something about the look in this older kid's eyes that told me this wasn't a joke. They surrounded me, and I felt I had no choice. I was suddenly experiencing a little panic. With the utmost reluctance and reservation, I placed my hand down on the stump. I thought, *if I can just get through this, it will be over and we can get back to having fun.* I put my hand down with my fingers splayed out on the stump. I watched him as he took the hatchet from another kid. I thought *maybe he's just trying to scare me, and he's really not going to do it.* I waited. I watched his every move. My adrenalin was high, and my heart was thumping in my chest. Then he raised the hatchet and paused a moment. I was tense, watching, waiting. Every muscle in my body was tight, ready to move at his first flinch. Then, he swung. The hatchet came down hard and fast. There was no hesitation in his movement. I pulled my hand away just in time. The hatchet went "thwack," as it buried itself in the wood, echoing the sound of a loud thud. I just stood there blinking. Had I not moved my hand, I would certainly have lost my fingers. I couldn't believe it! I was still processing it all. *He was actually going to do it!* Now I knew that the situation was more dire than I could have imagined.

The sun was getting low, and the shadows were getting long. The boys began to assert that I had moved my hand too quickly. For that reason it wasn't good enough. It didn't count. Their faces were dark, backlit by the fading sun. They insisted that I put my hand down again. When I perceived that they were not going to be satisfied until I lost some fingers, I took off running. The boys gave chase. I ran down the main trail looking for cover. My pulse was racing. I ran as fast as my legs could carry me. Up and down small hills I raced through bushes and around trees, my face and arms repeatedly whipped by branches and brambles. I didn't stop. I didn't look back. I left the main trail and ran down a narrow path. I moved through a rabbit trail. I hung a left. I took off down another obscure trail again trying to lose them. I ran quickly, looking anywhere for a place to hide. I came over the brow of a hill and tripped on some rocks. I pitched forward and fell down a steep grade sliding into a pile of dead leaves. I looked up, spitting out dirt. An old man with a fishing pole was standing in the shallows of a large pond. He wore high rubber boots and was casting his line into the water.

He smiled with surprise and said, "Well, you took quite a slip there, fella. You ok?" I was frantic. I stood up breathing hard. I looked around and back up the trail I came from. There was nobody behind me. "There is a Scout troop chasing me, and they're trying to kill me! They want to chop my fingers off!" I said, practically breathless.

He just laughed like he didn't believe me. I kept looking back. The boys were gone. They likely had seen the old man and then decided to head back to camp. I waited there by the old fisherman until, out of good faith or obligation, I couldn't tell which, he walked with me back to camp. When he saw that I was safely delivered, and that the boys had adult supervision, he said goodnight and left. Our weekend campout was only a two-nighter, so I made a point to stick close to the Scoutmaster for the rest of the weekend. Later, when we returned from camp, I told my mother what had happened. The next day I quit the troop. But I had had an encounter with evil that I would never forget. And it certainly wouldn't be my last encounter.

Evil also stalked me in the form of the Stogel gang. Johnny Stogel and his buddies were relentless in their harassment. Johnny was a tough, aggressive kid. He and his friends' favorite pastime was making my life miserable. I would sit in class, analyzing my various options for walking home to avoid getting beaten by them.

Let's see....The way I see it there are only three alternative ways of getting home, three possible options...one: hitch a ride home with a friend's parent... Oh, that's right...no friends.

Two: I could just jump the freeway fence and follow the green space all the way to my house.

My school was built along the freeway. My house was also on a cul-de-sac near the same freeway. It occurred to me that if I could jump the chain-link fence in back of the school, I could hike near the freeway shrubs along the fence until I came to my cul-de-sac. Then I could hop the fence again. Voila'! I would be home! The six foot fence, however, proved to be more than a challenge for my ten year old frame. That wasn't going to work for the long haul.

Or, there was the third choice. Instead of walking home the usual half mile route, I could go in the opposite direction, taking a very wide two and a half mile loop, eventually getting back to my house.

I opted for the longer walk home. This option, of course, required me to walk two and a half miles daily instead of the customary half mile home, and I would need to explain the time differential to my mother. No problem. I would just lie and tell her that I had been visiting at a friend's house. Problem solved! I started taking the long way home, and for a while this worked. However, even this tactic proved to be impractical as I got tired of walking the unnecessary distance every day. What choice did I have, though? To do otherwise would mean that I would be mercilessly hunted down like prey. I was living Darwin's law of the jungle: it was survival of the fittest, and the weak were shown no mercy. I perceived that no matter where I went or what I tried to do, evil seemed to be stalking me.

These circumstances began to have a significant impact on my school work. I routinely brought home poor grades on my progress reports, provoking the wrath of my dad who understandably wanted all his kids to perform well and be successful. My dad used the punishment and rewards system. For example, for good grades our dad would give us money and lavish us with praise. If we brought home bad grades we would get some form of punishment. This punishment usually came in the form of some action designed to put the fear of God in me. Restrictions ensued, along with corporal punishment, and late night yelling sessions over my homework and lack of comprehension of fractions and word problems. My fear only increased as I convinced myself that I lacked the faculties to think and reason mathematically.

I continued to be unable to concentrate in class. My fifth grade teacher grew impatient as my mind would drift into the outer reaches of time and space. I dreaded parent/teacher conferences. The thought of my parents and teacher in the same room with me at the same time terrified me. Talk about a nightmare come true! All this pressure began to take its toll on me. It mounted to such a degree that I felt as though it just might crush me. In the fifth grade I had a nervous breakdown the day before a parent/teacher conference. The moment felt surreal. I broke down crying in the middle of class, and the teacher gave me a time-out so I could collect myself outside. Something significant happened at that moment. Something inside me snapped. I had come to the end of myself. I had figured out that nothing could be more stressful or painful than what I was experiencing at that moment. It was this epiphany that caused the shift in my thinking. Now I was feeling anger, not an emotion that I was familiar with at the time. I had never allowed myself to get angry, but I was angry now. It wasn't anger just toward one individual. It was more generalized then that. I was angry at the evil that had been harassing me continually. I was angry at the injustice of it all, and I was finally determined to do something about it. Something changed in me, and the change was irreversible.

CHAPTER 2

The Tipping Point

THE TIPPING POINT IS THE critical moment in any given situation that leads to the point of no return, resulting in a new outcome. It's the crossing of a threshold, a turning point, often the accumulation of relatively small things that make the major difference. I can't say what specifically made the difference for me. But I do know that it was a culmination of events that made the fear I was experiencing unbearable.

At the end of my fifth grade year I was finally tired of being afraid all the time. All the combined fear and stress from my parent's rocky marriage, the expectation of their possible divorce, the drinking and instability at home, the pressure of getting good grades to avoid my dad's wrath, and all the threats at school finally brought me to my limit. All the pressure, fear, and stress brewing inside me since the first grade began to bubble up into a seething cauldron of rage just beneath the surface of my being. I had reached my limit, and I didn't care anymore. Some call it the tipping point. At that moment, I became the proverbial volcano waiting to erupt.

It was a warm day in May. I was standing in the playground by the lunch benches when the Stogel kid and his buddies approached and started threatening me. The threat came with Johnny pointing his finger in my face while saying something like, "You just wait; you're dead after school!" That was the popular line he liked to use. I normally would have crumbled in the face of such a threat. Strangely, for the first time I was unmoved. I answered Johnny by saying, "You'd better be there!" Of course I knew that he would be there, along with his buddies and a crowd of kids as word got around school. My anxiety continued to build throughout the day as I realized that these three boys were going to be waiting for me when school ended. Again, I was learning the law of the jungle where only the strong survive, and the weak are ultimately destroyed.

I spent the whole day watching the clock, anticipating the bell. This made it impossible for me to focus or concentrate in class. I wasn't hearing a word the teacher was saying. If someone had put a gun to my head and asked me to repeat what the teacher had said, I'm sure that I would most certainly be dead. My adrenaline was pumping; my heart was beating out of my chest. This would be my first real fight, ever. This time I would fight back. I spent the rest of the day on pins and needles... waiting.

After school got out, I started walking home. I was determined to end this thing. When I finally came to the end of the school's chain-link fence, Johnny and his buddies came out from behind the bushes and got in my face. That was it! All hell broke loose! Like the hammer in a gun striking the firing pin, a charge was ignited. All the pressure that had been building, all my fear, stress, fury, and rage reached its peak. Like a stick of dynamite I exploded on Johnny and those boys. Though I didn't know how to fight, I just kept swinging. Johnny was a skilled fighter. He kept ducking under my swings. I kept throwing round-house punches at him. I started to land a few punches to his face. The other boys were caught by surprise. They didn't know what to do. I had never fought back before. They immediately backed off. Johnny and I continued to fight, and though I kept getting hit in the face, I didn't feeling any pain (adrenaline is a wonderful thing). Johnny started to back off. All the commotion from the kids around us didn't go unnoticed by the faculty, however. Next thing I knew, we were being pulled apart by our collars and taken to Mr. Morris's office. They called our homes, and we were promptly suspended for the next day and sent home. This would be my first suspension.

Words cannot adequately describe what I was feeling as I walked home that day. I was weightless, even euphoric! The total release of all that built-up pressure and stress was suddenly replaced by euphoria and a sense of peace. I felt so light; I was floating. All I knew was that I had never felt better. This nirvanic state was soon tainted by the afterthought of what would be waiting for me when my dad got home that evening. I knew the punishment would be severe with a lot of yelling thrown in for good measure, and it was.

When I finally returned to school, I walked with my head held high and with two black eyes. When Johnny saw me, he approached me sporting only one black eye and wearing a big smile on his face. Then he extended his hand toward me in what was at least a truce, if not friendship. We shook hands and became friends from that point on. The other kids slapped my back, giving me a lot of kudos and atta-boys. Suddenly, kids who had never given me the time of day knew my name. All this attention only served to reinforce my behavior. I found that several needs were met in my fight with Johnny: emotional release, attention, and respect. I determined that I would never back down from a fight ever again. I didn't yet realize that I was giving permission for evil to come back and challenge me again and again. Ironically, the fear I thought I conquered gave rise to an even greater adversary.

My sixth grade year brought cocky, loud mouthed, Calen Finn into my life. He was a red-haired trouble maker. Name-calling, mocking, and bullying were some of Calen's favorite pastimes. His mother thought that he could do no wrong. Once, during recess, Calen's mother could be heard yelling at the staff in the administration office. He was a huge problem, and all the teachers knew it. He was even suspended for punching *a teacher* in the stomach once. When he began to focus on me for his amusement, I wasn't about to stand for it. The day he challenged me, we immediately went to blows. We wrestled around on the ground, kicking each other until a teacher finally pulled us apart, sweaty, grassy, and breathing heavy. When we got up off the ground, Calen had a huge bump egging out from under his eye. Once again I was in the principal's office, and according to the school policy it didn't matter who was at fault. Both of us were sent home and told not to return to school the following day. However, just as I was leaving the office, the receptionist gave me a wink on my way out the door. To say that my dad was not pleased would have been a huge understatement. He went ballistic! He raged and yelled for a good hour. Then I was restricted to my room for two weeks.

I returned to school a day later and received affirmation and praise from all the kids. I was now getting the attention I desperately craved. From that point on I fought at every possible opportunity. *Never again will I ever put up with another jerk getting in my face or threatening me!* Moreover, the opportunities to fight abounded. It seemed that there was never a shortage of punks wanting to get their lights punched out. They were practically lining up! If I had charged money, I would've been rich! It wasn't that I was looking for a fight or even wanted the conflict. Quite honestly, fighting was contrary to my nature. It just seemed that wherever I went, trouble always seemed to find me. It was as though I had been marked by some underground organization to be rubbed out! It would be years later before I would find out how true that was.

Almost immediately after starting junior high school, I was sent home after a fight and a suspension. My dad insisted that I was starting these fights. I tried to explain that it wasn't my fault and that others were always starting them. My dad just yelled, "Right! It's never *your* fault!" I wondered why it seemed that everyone wanted to fight *me. Why is it that evil always seemed to be stalking me?* Little did I know I would learn the real answer to that question in my adult years. I later learned that many of the other kids had not experienced even one major conflict throughout their whole school life. I thought: *How is that possible?* I wondered what was so different about me. I was mystified. Regardless, I continued to fight all the way through junior high school, and was sent home on two more occasions, much to my parents' dismay. I thought high school might be different.

At the end of summer, football season was approaching. Tryouts were starting, and I was beginning my freshmen year of high school. I had absolutely no intention of ever playing football. My dad was a big "sporto," and it was always important to him that I play sports. What was so ironic was that I had absolutely no interest in sports. However, I played baseball up to this point for only two reasons: 1) my dad's strong encouragement to play, and 2) my dad's approval. For these reasons I played little league baseball every year during my childhood.

My true interest was not in sports but in the outdoors. This became obvious even when I was small. Once during a baseball game when I was playing center field, I noticed on the ground a bunch of red ants attacking a grasshopper. I could see that they were in the process of dismembering the insect to carry it into their burrow. Fascinated and fully engrossed, I was caught up in the whole drama. As I leaned in closer with my forearms resting on my knees, I could almost hear the grasshopper faintly screaming for help...actually screaming at me... "Help! Help! Help! Hey! Hey! Get the ball! GET THE BALL!" I finally looked up to see a crowd of people jumping up and down screaming at me to get the ball! I was completely oblivious to the fact that a fly ball had just whizzed past me. All I could think at that moment was: *CRAP! A fly ball just went over my head!* Needless to say, I never made it to the major leagues.

Now I was in Bolsa Grande High School. It was a large school with red, white, and blue as its colors. With elongated red-brick construction, the school was built with its administration offices near the center of the front parking lot. Behind those offices were two rows of classrooms with lockers and concrete walkways. To the left was a large gymnasium along with the men's and women's locker rooms. In back of the gym was a small blacktop with a large expanse of grass beyond that. Our football stadium was located in the back of the school to the left of our large grassy field.

In the 1980's, punk, new wave, and classic rock music ruled the airwaves. Like most high schools, Bolsa Grande's student body was divided by the various sub-cultures. The jocks, cheerleaders, and ASB people all hung out in the center of school claiming a short two-foot brick wall. Near the gym, you would always find the biker, hessian, stoner crowd in a circle on the grass. Then there were the Vietnamese students who hung out under a tree and more or less kept to themselves. Loners, geeks and those considered the odds-and-ends of the school populace usually stayed in the library. I was a loner trying to be a jock. It was never my intention to be a jock; it just worked out that way.

My first year of high school I was six feet tall and one hundred and forty pounds soaking wet. One day prior to football hell-week and the start of the semester, my dad took me to get a high school physical examination. I didn't want it. I protested, but he insisted. I'm sure he just wanted me checked out by the physician to make sure my health and my head were okay after so many scuffles over the years. I went in reluctantly. Standing there, I waited in line to see the physician so I could turn my head and cough.

I had no intention of playing football. I was thin as a rail, and I had never played football. As I waited in the locker room, a number of my peers laughed at the idea that I was even there. The dialogue went something like this:

"Jacques, what are you doing here?"

"I'm here to get a physical," I said.

"This is only for guys trying out for football." Attitude like *what the hell are you thinkin'?*

"I *am* signing up for football!" I asserted.

"Then what position are you trying out for?"

"I don't know yet!" I countered.

"You have no idea what's going on, do you Jacques?"

I made no comment to that. I had no clue about any of the positions. I had played baseball my whole life. Later, I discreetly talked to someone who told me that they were trying out for defensive end and explained the position to me. Once I understood what a defensive end did, from that point on, any time I was asked, I would say that I was trying out for defensive end.

These guys knew my history, that I had never played football. Many of them grew up playing together. Consequently, they made great efforts to make sure that I remained in the tiny box I had been relegated to. So, they launched a protest about me trying out. I was having none of it. Now this only made me more determined to play. *Nobody is going to tell me what I can or can't do! I'll show them! I am playing in spite of them!* However, I was too light for a lineman, and lacked the experience for the other more skilled positions. I reasoned that I could just figure it out as I go. I returned to the car and gave my dad the pleasant surprise that I had signed up for the football team. He just smiled and said, "All right!" What he didn't know was that *I* was as surprised as he was.

School had started, and some of the players who knew me resented me wanting to play. One football player, Greg Phil, decided to pick a fight with me during my freshman year. This kid knew me from grade school and thought he was going to discourage me from playing. He was two inches taller than I was. He stood nose to nose with me to emphasize his height advantage, taunting me. Then he grabbed me by the front of my shirt collar, pushing me up against the brick-wall of the building. That was it! I unloaded a flurry of punches to his face. It was so fast that I must have stunned him. He let go and backed way off. We were both suspended from school that day, and he would have nothing to do with me afterwards. Problem solved.

That, of course, did not solve my problems at home. As a family, we stopped going to Catholic church after my last year of junior high school. It was right after my sisters and I made our first Holy Communion and our Confirmation. These ceremonies, similar to a school graduation, were all very academic to me. It wasn't until my dad and mom stopped taking us to church that I began to see visible signs of their marriage deteriorating. I believe it was the little influence the church was having on my parents that was keeping their marriage and our family together. Still, there was some force at work in our family, pulling us apart.

It was the disintegration of my parent's marriage that made high school a lot more stressful. I felt that my future was more uncertain, like I was flying on a trapeze without a net. Consequently, I used football as a distraction from all that was going on at home. I became a master of distraction. Ironically, despite my best efforts to prove myself and gain acceptance from my peers, I failed miserably. I was benched for most of football season. My grades were nominal to my dad's utter disappointment, and I continued to attract a violent element. Overall, I felt like a miserable failure. I felt less than, odd, different from everybody else, like I was always on the outside looking in. I tried to act tough and keep it together, but inside I felt completely inadequate, isolated and alone. Worse yet, the violent evil that had stalked me through my primary school years still plagued me. And I was at a loss to know why or how it could ever change.

In my high school years my parents were drifting apart. Alcohol and drinking increased in our home, and arguments were replaced by longer workdays for dad and less time together as a family. Somehow I managed to maintain a C average in school. This grade point average still allowed me to play football, which my parents continued to support. It was a very dark season in my life, and I experienced increased anxiety as I anticipated my parents' pending divorce. The prospect of their possible separation continually loomed over me like a black thunder cloud waiting to strike at any moment. Home became characteristically more depressing, the atmosphere more tainted with drinking and alcohol. Our family's relationships became increasingly disengaged. Consequently, home changed into an unpredictable place. Coming home from school, I never knew what I was walking into. Sometimes, I would come home to find mom in mid-celebration with friends and entertaining a few strangers standing at the kitchen bar. They would all have cigarettes and drinks in their hands. It was then that I knew it was going to be a long night. Other times the feeling at home was tense and uncomfortable, like something bad could happen at any moment. I knew that things were not as they should be, and it tormented me. I wanted to distance myself from the pain of my deteriorating family, and I wanted to push everyone away.

Fear and anxiety had plagued me before, but now it was masked by anger. I felt lonely, like I didn't fit in anywhere, and I was mad at the world. It was about that time that I became aware of a deeper hunger in my life, though I couldn't identify it at the time. I began to search for something not knowing what I was looking for.

I was well into my sophomore year of high school when I was suspended after another fight. I still hadn't figured out why I seemed to have this big target painted on my forehead. What was it about me that made every kid inclined toward violence want to challenge me? Maybe it was my demeanor and the way I carried myself, or maybe it was something else altogether. Whatever it was, I didn't seem to be growing out of it. Before I knew it, I was facing another challenger. Manny was a punk rocker, as mean and full of rage as any kid I had ever met. He had cold, blue eyes, and his blond hair had been buzzed on top. He was short, stocky and full of attitude. It was in the locker room that we first crossed paths.

The locker room was filled with the smell of sweat mixed with a warm, thick shower mist. Sounds of hollering and the slamming of lockers reverberated off the tiled walls and concrete floors. The fight started when I passed by Manny's locker. As though given some silent cue, he decided to come after me. Why? I had no idea. But we "threw-down" there in the locker room. I was a reasonably confident fighter by that time. However, he charged and tackled me to the concrete floor. I lacked the bodyweight to stay standing. In our initial altercation he got the best of me. I took a couple of hits to the mouth, and began to get the metallic taste of blood. Guys were standing all around us whooping it up and yelling. One of the coaches finally broke it up. The coach must have thought the fight was over because when things settled down he left the room again. Manny just pointed his finger at me promising he was going to finish the fight after school. Well, that was the *wrong* thing to say, because I was thinking, *Ok, I can fight this guy right now, and get it over with, or I can ride the anxiety train all day waiting for school to end... I'm going to fight him now!* So, I walked back over to Manny's side of the locker room and yelled in the loudest, most threatening voice I could muster, "If you want to fight me, you fight me now!"

I was a better fighter than I was a wrestler. Manny was shorter but heavier and didn't have my reach. However, someone had taught him well. The first thing he did was tackle me again. My back slammed against the lockers. We slid to the floor. Wrestling put me at a significant disadvantage. He was on top of me, but I had him jacked up on my knees. Intense hatred was in his eyes, like a man possessed. I could see his hair was buzzed on top and long on the sides, so I grabbed hold of those blond locks with my left hand. I continued to hang onto his hair as I punched upward from the ground at his face. I was definitely landing a few, because his left eye started swelling. Guys were yelling all around us, and it became quite the scene. When the coach broke us up for the second time, we were sent straightaway to the school office. After a good talking-to, we were asked to shake hands. We both gave the obligatory hand shake and were promptly suspended from school. I left and walked home with several knots on my head. I vaguely remember getting home and my mom being very sympathetic and concerned. I don't think she knew how to change the violent course of my life, but I knew that she was hurting inside because of me.

In my junior year of high school I went to my first (and last) high school party. It was in a tract home, and I didn't even know the owner. All I knew was there would be lots of girls and a kegger of beer. The irony was that I hated the whole party scene. I had experienced the party scene at home enough to know that it usually didn't end well. People seemed to lose all inhibitions and any sense of what is appropriate when alcohol was present. I remember a fist fight breaking out at our house one time and an unwelcome advance from a much older woman on another occasion.

On the other hand, my mom always intended such events to be a celebration. Mom loved to dance, and she would often blare songs from Neil Diamond's "Hot August Night" while busting a move with her friends. It was all in good fun, but I was very uncomfortable with the whole scene. I would often spend those nights hunkered down in my bedroom listening to muffled sounds of droning music and gaiety.

Nevertheless, there I was walking into some stranger's house with blaring music and a crowd of people that I didn't know. I meandered through this living room full of people, feeling utterly alone. As I stood there scanning the smoke-filled living room, (smoking was still cool back then) looking at the different faces and the half-closed eyelids at this slush fest, I couldn't help but think: *Wow! This whole scene is just pathetic.* I decided not to stay, so I left to go get a cheeseburger at the closest fast food joint.

My junior year was the same year that the older of my two sisters started dating someone that I suspected was a drug dealer. He seemed shady and liked to keep to himself and away from the family. Being an older brother I was naturally concerned. My sister was someone people refer to as a strong-willed child, and from birth she was at war with the world. She was the type who had to learn everything firsthand, in her own way. Nobody was going to tell her how to do *anything*. My sister and I were one year apart, and we fought like we were on the opposite sides of a blood-feud. It seemed to me that she would have it no other way but, truth be told, I was also guilty of stoking the fires of her fury. Still, I felt an unwavering responsibility to protect her. Consequently, I would take out my aggression on campus.

It was on campus that I fought with a kid by the name of Ron Matley. Ron had a height advantage on me as well as twenty more pounds of bulk. That wasn't the worst of it. He was also trained in martial arts. I was clearly outmatched, but I actually thought I could take him. I thought, *Isn't it peachy? All those years that I was playing baseball, this kid was training, learning the fine art of hand-to-hand combat.* I suppose all those years of baseball might have helped me if I had only had a baseball bat in my hands, but I didn't.

Ron was a tall kid with a smug look and a wave in his hair. Moreover, he carried himself with an attitude of superiority. The fight took place by the school gym, near the boys' locker room... again! You'd have thought I'd start to realize that a locker room was a bad place to hang out. Nonetheless, there I was when Ron decided to pick a fight with me. I don't remember the reason for the fight. Come to think of it, I don't think there was a reason. Maybe he wanted to test his martial art skills. Whatever the reason, he decided to grab my shirt. Touch had always been my limit line. Once someone touched me, that was it! I wasn't about to wait to see what happens next. So when Ron touched me, I threw everything I knew at him. My adrenaline was high. My heart was racing. I gave him a flurry of punches. I threw a right, a left. Then a right again. It was all happening so fast; it was a blur. I continued punching at his face. I wasn't landing anything. His arms were up deflecting my every punch. He effectively blocked my every move. He, on the other hand, landed every punch; at least it felt like that after we were pulled apart and it was all over. We were both taken to the school office by faculty and suspended. Again, it didn't matter who started it, or whose fault it was. We were both suspended for two days.

On the way home from the fight, I really started to pay the price. As I walked, I came down off my adrenaline high. My whole head began pounding. The headache was excruciating. As I reached up holding my head in my hands, I could feel lumps (subdural hematomas) all over my face and head. It was the worst fight I had ever experienced, and in the aftermath I knew that I was hurting badly.

That's when I uttered my first real prayer. Tears began to fill my eyes as I cried to God for the first time. "God, I'm so tired of fighting. I don't want to fight anymore." When I got home, I took three aspirins and went to bed. I could see the hurt and pain that my mother was feeling for me, but neither she nor I knew how to change the violent pattern in my life.

Time passed, and my junior year came and went, my prayer long forgotten. It was during the month of July that a kid who lived down the street from me started yelling at me. I was walking home from the drugstore when he called out to me from the street corner, a stalky Hispanic kid with a buzz cut. While shooting daggers with his eyes, he bowed his arms with his chest out and kept mouthing the words to me, "Come on! Come on!" He continued egging me on for a fight, and I was more than willing to oblige him. I crossed the street to meet him. When I confronted him, he pulled a knife and held it down by his side. Since he had an unfair advantage, I had no qualms about turning around and walking away. He didn't come after me, so I just went home.

Later that day, however, he came after my sister and she told me about it. That was it. I went hunting for him. I was halfway down the street when he saw me. Immediately, he came and faced off with me. There was no knife this time. Instantly, I had this kid down on the ground in a headlock, after punching him several times. Blood was pouring out of his mouth and nose onto the sidewalk as his face began to turn purple in my chokehold. After I felt I had gotten my point across to leave my sister alone, I let him go. *Communication is a wonderful thing.* There was never a problem with him afterwards.

My senior year of high school I had been lifting weights, swimming, and downing protein shakes all summer. I had gained five pounds. I went from a puny one hundred and forty pounds to a one hundred and forty five pound stud monster! And I held myself accordingly, walking with a slightly exaggerated swagger. No one would ever best me again. (Self-perception can be amazingly deceptive). One rainy day, I was walking out the back of the gym locker rooms to cross the back lot of the school. There, I usually went through the fence and walked home. On this day, before I could get to the fence, another kid challenged me to a fight. This kid's name was Kevin. He was about my height, but he wasn't very big, nor did he look that strong. However, Kevin was a blond, cocky, football player loaded with arrogance. He was one of the cool, popular, kids and was in the starting line-up on our football team. He always had lots of friends around him and a mouth that just wouldn't shut up.

On this occasion, when I came out of the locker rooms, I saw Kevin waiting for me out on the grass, I recognized trouble, so I put down my gym bag. The dialogue went something like this: "I don't want to fight you, Kevin." "What's wrong? Are you chicken? Here chick, chick, chick," Kevin harassed, as he started to bob in and out circling me. I said nothing. I just kept turning and kept facing him with my arms up ready to fight if necessary. "Come on! Fight, chicken! Fight, chicken! Come on!" A small crowd gathered in the rain to watch the spectacle. Kevin continued taunting. Then he tried to throw a punch. The punch was weak and didn't really connect. Then I fired three hard punches to his face, a one-two-three combination. He just stopped and stood there stunned... still...silent...staring. I was amazed his nose wasn't bleeding. The small group remained unusually quiet. Without turning my back on him and his friends, I just picked up my gym bag, backed away, and went home. He never bothered me again, and as far as I was concerned, that was my end-game.

===== CHAPTER 3 =====

Directionless

IT WAS ALL VERY ANTI-CLIMATIC. High school graduation was supposed to be a big deal, but the event was overshadowed by a sense that something was terribly wrong. Dad and Mom certainly tried to make it special and took me out to dinner. I had graduated with a flying D average. I hated school, and when I finally got my diploma, I felt like a man just released from a four year prison sentence. No longer would I be forced to spend another day trapped in that hostile environment. I was finally free to do what I wanted, when I wanted. The joy that came with my new sense of freedom was also tainted by feelings of ambivalence. I couldn't have been happier than to be out of school. However, I kept being taunted in the back of my mind by a question that would not leave me alone. The question was simply: *What now?*

It wasn't long after I graduated that my parents filed for divorce. My stomach sank when I heard the news. This was the day I had been dreading and hoping would never come. I walked around feeling very depressed, betrayed, lonely, abandoned, and directionless. I had no particular interest in anything. After such a negative experience with school, I had no intention of ever going to college unless, of course, I was shot and dragged there. Life overall seemed meaningless. My zest for life had been snuffed out by what I considered to be the death of my family. *What now?*

My first job was in a fast food joint flipping and serving burgers in the Westminster mall. It took me no time at all to realize that I wasn't cut out for food service. However, I liked my co-workers, and we had a lot of fun hanging out after work that summer. I was eighteen years old and an emotional wreck, full of anger and rage, although I was not consciously aware of it. I understand that when a person is extremely broken it's often hard for them to see the forest for the trees. I was no exception. I was completely unaware of my own pain and dysfunction. I was very cut off from my emotions, desperately seeking identity and direction.

I committed myself to seeking escape and distraction, and it was in this season of life that I began to dabble in pornography. An acquaintance had introduced me to some of his dad's magazines, and we would peruse them when his parents weren't home. We had even gone to an adult theater on one occasion, and I quickly became addicted to lust. Like the violence in my past, I had unknowingly opened another doorway to evil. I thought porn to be harmless. It would be years later before I would learn about the very real dangers associated with pornography.

It was the summer after I turned nineteen that I got a job with an older guy named Marvin. Marvin was a tile setter, and I became his go-fer. As his go-fer, I was responsible to run tools back and forth from the truck to the worksite and mix and haul mud and grout. This kept me in shape, and I gained another ten pounds, weighing in at 165. It was backbreaking work, but the money was good. Better yet, I didn't have to work fast food anymore. Laying tile was not a full-time gig though, so I got a second job working at a machine shop in the early morning hours. Marvin had a wild side, but he was smart, funny and a lot of fun. He had a very rough and crude sense of humor which I found amusing. Marv's philosophy was work hard, play hard. He liked to drink, smoke and womanize, and we would blare his stereo listening to Boston, Van Halen and Def Leopard while enroute to the next work site.

Marvin took me under his wing and became like a big brother to me. He also had a couple of other friends, Ron and

Mick, who enjoyed many of the same things Marvin did with one added bonus: they loved to brawl. It seemed anytime we were out suckin' down a few brewskis, Ron and Mick would pick a fight with someone. This tendency toward violence was not something I was real keen about since I had just gotten out of the high school fight scene. Nonetheless, we had agreed to back each other up if a fight ever went down. I only realized later what a foolish alliance I had made. Still, I liked hanging out with them because life seemed to be one continuous adrenaline rush. In the back of my mind I knew these guys were trouble, but I tried to keep myself from getting in too deep with them. I failed.

One time Marvin offered me a toke from his joint (he also liked to smoke pot). The conversation that followed went something like this:

Marvin: "Aren't you even curious what it feels like?"

Me: "DUDE! I don't believe in breathing smoke into your lungs!" (After all, I had my standards)

Marvin: "Well, what if I made some brownies? Would you try it then?"

Me: "Yeah sure, I'll try it in a brownie."

Marvin: "Ok, I'll make some right now."

We then jumped in Marvin's truck, went to the store, and got a box of brownie mix. When we got back to Marvin's apartment, he mixed a large baggie of his wacky weed in a six cup tray of brownie mix and baked it. I had never tried marijuana or any other drug before, nor have I since. I was very naïve. I didn't realize that the effect of ingesting three pot brownies would be exponentially more potent than merely smoking it.

The next thing I remember, I was at a bowling alley watching Marvin play asteroids on a video monitor. The sound of balls knocking pins down echoed in the background. Loud music played, lights danced and bells rang as pinball games entertained their occupants. I was in such a fog that I was trying to sleep with my forehead pressed up against the side of the video game. I couldn't keep my eyes open. Marvin was unphased, probably because he was doing cocaine as well. He was annoyed by my behavior in a public place. He elbowed me hard and told me to stop acting like an idiot. I walked slowly out into the bowling alley in a daze thinking that I might curl up on the carpet and go to sleep. I came extremely close to doing just that. Fortunately, I still had enough conscious thought to realize that if I had curled up in a fetal position on the carpet in the middle of the bowling alley, someone might think it a little odd. My better sense won out...barely. Instead, I went back to where Marvin was playing asteroids and asked him for the keys to his truck so I could sleep it off. He gave me the keys, and I slept until he woke me up in front of my house. It was late at night, and my mom was in bed, so I went in and tried to sleep it off.

I set my alarm because I knew at zero four-thirty I had to be up, dressed and standing in front of my house. I always waited to be picked up for a day's work at the machine shop. The guy who had helped me secure the job would pick me up in the morning and drop me off at night.

As soon as he saw me, he asked, "What's wrong with you?" "I just had a late night, that's all," I said. That morning the foreman (my boss) knew something was *very* wrong with me. My eyes were red, and my movements were somewhat inhibited. This was a serious issue because the machining we did left little tolerance for error. It was an exacting process and mistakes were very costly to the company. After a clear demonstration that I was unable to function in a satisfactory way, I was called into the office, given my last check, and promptly fired.

Again, I was directionless. I continued working with Marvin through the following summer, and I was still partying with the boys. One night I was visiting a friend. It was late and we were sitting on the grass in front of his house. I had my legs crossed and was resting against my arms looking up at the stars when I started to ask him some deeper questions, questions I had been asking myself.

I began to think out loud, "Is this what it's going to be like for the rest of our lives? Is this what life is all about, just one endless cycle? Are we just going to party and get drunk every weekend, so we can work all week, earn a paycheck, so we can just party and get drunk again the following weekend? Is that it? Is that all there is to life?" "Don't you think there has to be something more than this?"

"I guess so. What else is there?" was my friend's simple reply to my questions.

It was a passing thought, but one that would begin to tug at me again and again. I could keep my deeper thoughts at bay as long as I kept myself distracted and busy, but inevitably I would begin again to contemplate the meaning of it all. Life just seemed too simplistic and pointless, and it bothered me. After all the parties are over, what's next? *What now?*

CHAPTER 4

Glimmer of Hope

THIS SEARCH FOR MEANING AND purpose continued to bother me like a fly buzzing around my head. I started to analyze the question, *"What is life all about?"* It led me to ask an even deeper, more pointed question, *What is MY life all about?* This question was much more personal, and it made me restless. My lack of direction began to plague me. I desperately needed some kind of focus. I came to the conclusion that what I needed was a plan for my life, and I spent a significant amount of time cogitating a plan. I didn't feel competent to do much, and I had no intention of ever going back to school. I didn't feel passionate about anything. I always found it difficult to do anything I didn't feel passionate about, but I felt as though all the passion had been drained out of me. I knew that I needed something, but I wasn't sure what that something was.

I was still searching for purpose and meaning. I knew that I needed some direction, a goal of some kind. I continued thinking, brainstorming. At first there seemed to be very little creative rain in the realm of ideas. Then it came to me...an idea. It was just an idea at first, but the more I thought about it, the more excited I got. Finally, I realized what I was going to do. I would go through the police academy and become a police officer! Finally, I knew! I just knew! My mind was made up. This was something that would give me focus and direction. I immediately went out and bought one of those thick police basic skills test booklets. I knew there was a police academy in Huntington Beach, so I started looking into it. I learned that there were two basic parts to the POST academy. Each part would take three months in its entirety. I determined that I would apply for the following cycle.

Before applying to the academy I was spending some time at a friend's house, a different friend this time. This friend's name was David, same as mine. David's parents lived in a very clean-looking, upscale neighborhood. David had a brother, Wayne, who shared my interest in the academy. He was also a motorhead, so we would stand around in his driveway as he worked on his car quizzing each other about different "what if" police scenarios. "What if you're walking up to a car to ticket someone, and you see suspicious movement in the front seat? What if you're called to a domestic disturbance, and the man of the house answers the door agitated and unwilling to let you in? What if you are called to arrest someone much bigger than you are and they are uncooperative, and you're alone?" So on and so on, we would go back and forth with questions for each other. This would be our discussion as he continued tinkering with his car.

It was during one such visit that David and I got on the subject of women. This was always an enjoyable topic. The topic had turned to the local and recent prospects when David abruptly invited me to a Bible study.

I said, "What? You mean a Bible study like at church?"
David: "Nah, they meet at a house."
Me: "No thanks, David. I've already done the church thing. Not interested."
David: "There will be a lot of cute girls there!"
Me: "Ok, you got me, I'll check it out. So when do they meet?"
David: "Tonight at seven."

I really was searching for something more in life. However, up to that point I hadn't found it at church. All I had known and experienced was a crowded cathedral with a bunch of strangers reciting meaningless liturgy.

I absolutely believed in God, theoretically, but the ritual that accompanied the Catholic mass seemed irrelevant to what I was experiencing in the real world. I never seemed to *get it*. The fact is, I didn't know anyone who actually lived the way they said you were supposed to. Nonetheless, I did have a genuine fascination with pretty girls, so I decided to go to the Bible study to check it out.

At that point I hadn't been to church in six years. That night I walked into a very warm-looking home with a fireplace. A man was leading worship, and about seventeen young people were gathered around on the carpet and in chairs singing. I was immediately struck by how inviting the atmosphere was. As my eyes panned the living room, I saw a group of young, glowing faces amidst the warm firelight. The youth pastor's name was Art, and after singing a number of songs about God and Jesus he began to open up the Bible and teach. The way this man talked about God peaked my interest. The study was completely absent of any kind of ritualism. The study was a dynamic, interactive discussion, and very personal, relevant issues were being discussed. I was expecting a history class, but these people were talking about God like they knew Him personally. This was nothing like what I had experienced before, and I wanted to hear more.

After the Bible study, I was warmly greeted by a number of very cute girls which only helped to secure my interest. The guys were cool and very nice as well. I had never in my life met kids so nice, and I was completely blown away. They immediately embraced and accepted me when I desperately needed acceptance. I was also a little leery. Having been raised Catholic, I had been taught the myth that anything outside Catholicism was not true Christianity. I determined that I wasn't going to be taken in by any cult. Each week after I attended this home Bible study, I would go home and compare the teachings to what I read in our huge, ten pound, Catholic family Bible. My family never opened it or read it. It was more of a living room ornament left on the coffee table by my late grandmother.

With every week that passed, I was more and more convinced that these people were for real and that, in fact, they were following the same God that I believed in. Moreover, these Christians, as they called themselves, were actually living it. Finally, I had a glimmer of hope that there was more to this life than what I had known. These Christians loved and accepted me, and I attended church any time the doors were open. They included me in all their activities. They even took me to a camp up in the mountains. I had never had so much fun in all my life, and the love they had for one another was evident to me. I thought to myself, *this is heaven on earth.* For the first time in my life I had friends, *real* friends, who actually cared about *me.* There was a sense of community and connection I had not experienced before. They became a surrogate family to me at a time when things were feeling very unstable at home. I remember wondering at the time, *Where have these people been all my life? I didn't know real Christians even existed!* Church became a haven of stability in my otherwise unstable and shifting world.

My dad had moved out of the house, and the rest of the family was not adjusting well to the change. Alcohol use shot up considerably in our family, and a shroud of darkness seemed to permeate the household. My mom had been a stay-at-home mother all of her married life, so when my dad left she was in somewhat of a panic. I didn't understand or perceive this at the time, as I was too preoccupied with my own pain and turmoil. My mom always had the ability to make fast friends with people and found solace at a nearby bar she frequented. There she had established a number of relationships over time.

Often she would invite her friends over for a nightcap and some laughs. As was now the custom, my mom's friends would stand at the kitchen bar drinking, laughing it up and telling tall tales.

My two younger sisters began staying out later and later. When my mom tried to restrict my older sister, she would sneak out the window at night where she rendezvoused with her boyfriend. It all felt chaotic and out of order. It seemed my family was continuing to be systematically ripped apart, and I felt powerless to do anything about it. More than that, it tore me up to see it. Home was feeling like a sinking ship, and I didn't want to sink with it into its dark icy waters. I began to spend as much time away from home as possible.

I started attending church. My Christian friends were an island of comfort and stability in the midst of a storm of fear and uncertainty. They were bringing light into my world when all I could see was darkness. The church was a safe haven for me, with its chapel style structure and traditional look. When I walked inside, I found the interior carpeted with a soft, warm looking décor that had a calming effect on me. Typically, a number of people milled around a small lobby socializing. The scent of mixed perfumes hovered in the room. Music played inside the sanctuary. There was a pulpit and a silver-haired gal at the piano up front playing. When the pastor began to preach, everything he said resonated with me. It was as though my life was being laid bare. Everything I was hearing was readily applicable, and I began attending consistently. Six months later, at a Christmas Eve service in 1982, I went forward to ask Jesus Christ into my heart. I prayed, asking Him to forgive me for all my sins and to fill me with His Holy Spirit. It wasn't a decision I was taking lightly, and I was baptized that same evening.

That week something changed inside me. I knew it! I was different, and I could feel it. I couldn't have described it back then, but I had a warm peace, and a joy filling my heart that I had never felt before. All I knew was I was forgiven, and I felt so light. My conversion was dramatic, like flipping on a light switch, like going from seeing in black and white to seeing in color. I just knew that I had met God, and that He was with me. I was so excited, and so zealous, I began telling everyone about Jesus including my mom and my sisters. However, none of my family members could receive what I had to say. My mother, plagued with guilt and feelings of failure, did not feel worthy of anything God was offering. My siblings were not receiving what I had to say because of past hurts and unresolved conflict. I tried to apologize and to ask them for forgiveness, but I don't think they believed that I had really changed. When I tried to share Jesus with my dad, he got very angry that I had left the Catholic church. I tried to tell him that He was the same Jesus, but he didn't want to hear it. I was a new believer, and though I was zealous for God, I wasn't very sensitive to the feelings of others, least of all my parents.

I was in the honeymoon period of my Christianity, and it was glorious. I fell in love with God and the church, and I immediately discerned the differences between the atmosphere at home and the atmosphere at church. Church seemed so sound, safe, and stable, that I spent more and more time there. The environment at church was full of peace while my home life felt so chaotic and unstable. When I went home, I would literally feel a spiritual darkness in my house. The darkness was palpable. I remember my siblings and I being plagued by terrible nightmares when we were kids. We would go to my parents' room in tears, and mom would stay up and talk to us in the kitchen. After comforting us, she would send us back to bed. Now after the divorce, I really didn't feel I had a family anymore and it seemed all I was experiencing at home was pain. The church had become a stable and peaceful replacement for my family, filling a major gap in my life.

I had just turned twenty when I started the police academy. The first part involved twelve weeks of training and was called the POST Reserve Academy. There we learned the California Vehicle Code, the California Penal Code, and how to manage night problems and domestic disputes. We frequented the shooting range and learned arrest and control techniques. We did a lot of running, push-ups, and sit-ups, and even spent time being exposed to CS gas in a gas chamber. We later learned to drive defensively on the skid-pan. This is where you would have to learn to regain control of your vehicle in the event that you went into an uncontrolled skid.

Upon completion, the POST Reserve Academy qualifies a person to work as a reserve (part-time) police officer. The Extended-Format Academy provides another twelve weeks of training. Graduates from the Extended Format Academy are qualified to work as full-time police officers. I was two weeks away from graduation when it happened. The evil from my boyhood came back to haunt me.

I was home on the weekend when my sister's boyfriend (the suspected drug dealer) came to the door. I was sitting on the couch watching TV when he demanded, "Where's Chris?" Before I could answer, he let himself into our house and proceeded down the hallway. I started to seethe, feeling disrespected in my own house. I began to hear them fighting and arguing. They came back out through the living room and continued arguing out on the front porch in very loud voices.

My anger was now bubbling to the surface: *This guy let himself in without being invited! There is no respect for me or my sister.* A volcano was now churning inside me, ready to erupt. Then, I stood and went to the front door. I asked him what was going on. He retorted, "None of your business!"

That's it! I figured if it involved my sister it *was* my business. I went outside, stepped between them, and got nose to nose with this guy. Then I said, "What's your problem?" His eyes narrowed. He started yelling, pointing his finger in my face. The rest was a blur. Without thinking through the consequences of my actions, I unleashed my fury on this guy. He kicked at me a couple of times. His kicks landed on the side of my leg and were ineffective. I threw a right punch. The guy's nose exploded like a ripe tomato. Blood was everywhere, on his shirt, all over the porch. His nose was like a faucet. When it was all over, the guy was pulling out of the driveway with a broken nose. With fist raised, he yelled curses and threats out the window as he sped away.

Thirty minutes later, there was a knock at the door. When I answered it, two police officers stood there. The guy was there too, behind them, holding a towel over his nose. They asked me what happened, and I gave them a breakdown of the play-by-play series of events leading to the final altercation. When they learned that I was in the academy, and that their sergeant was my TI (Training Instructor), they tried to negotiate with this guy not to press charges. Their reasoning went something like: "Look, you're dating his sister. You don't want to alienate the family, do you? What if he agrees to pay the doctor bills? Will you agree to drop the charges?" In the end, the guy told the officers that he was insured, and that he would not press charges. Wow! That was a close call. It was then and there that it dawned on me that I was not in high school anymore, and that my actions could mean serious consequences for my future, not the least of which could mean time in the slammer!

When things finally settled down, I was extremely disappointed in myself. If I was trying to be any example of a Christian man, I realized that I had just blown it. My family would never take my faith seriously. They would assume that all my talk about faith in God was hollow, merely another phase, and that I would soon be moving on to the next *thing*. More than that, I had committed a major sin against God, and I was feeling grieved about it.

I had certainly dodged a bullet, a least that's what I thought at the time. What I didn't realize was that the police had taken a report, and that a copy of that report had found its way into the hands of my training instructor (TI). That Monday, I stood at parade rest, in formation with twenty other recruits. It was my last inspection, so we were all called to attention and remained in formation. The sun was hot, and each of us waited our turn as the TIs made their way down the row of recruits, checking our uniforms, and performing a thorough examination of our weapon to see if it was clean or not. It soon became obvious that my TI was privy to the previous weekend's incident because he stopped in front of me, grabbed my hand and examined my knuckles. There were several divots in my skin where I had hit the guy in the teeth. The jig was up, and I knew it. I was seriously sweating the situation. This altercation with my sister's boyfriend would prove to be a major issue.

I finished the reserve police academy, and my TIs graciously allowed me to walk, graduate, and receive my certificate of completion. However, they called me into their office after ceremonies, sat me down, and told me point blank, "We cannot recommend you for police work. We feel that you need more life experience before we could recommend you. Also, there were inconsistencies on your psychological evaluation. This tells us that you really don't know who you are yet. We advise you to get out. Get some life experience. Then come back later to complete the extended format academy." I thought to myself, *In other words, grow up first.*

I was devastated. Everything my TIs had said was true. I was extremely immature for my age, and I lacked good judgment and discretion. But I was still gravely disappointed. Much later in life I would learn that when children are raised in an addictive household they often forfeit the development of their own identity to take on a role. Role-playing insulates a child from pain by creating a wall around their true self; however, they do this at the cost of developing their true identity. This is something family members do unconsciously to survive an unpredictable, and sometimes, chaotic environment. It's a survival mechanism. Trauma can stop a child's emotional growth and development. This essentially keeps them stuck emotionally at the point at which they were traumatized. But as I said before, they do this at the expense of their emotional maturity. A person learns to take on a personality (or identity) like they would put on a coat, as long as it suits the moment. They become an onion with different layers of assumed identities to form what is essentially a false identity. I was a classic example of this. I was brand new in my Christian faith. The conflict between wanting to be like Dirty Harry and Jesus Christ at the same time was obviously incongruent. It was this lack of identity that impacted my psychological evaluation. I would assume an identity for whatever I thought would fit the moment, like a chameleon, but with no real sense of self.

I was crushed. My glimmer of hope had been snuffed out. My search for direction, affirmation, and identity had been cut short, and I was in a tailspin of disappointment and depression. Hope deferred certainly makes the heart sick, and I was feeling sick to my stomach. Worse yet, I was supposed to be living as a committed Christian. I felt like a failure, and felt that I really disappointed God and let Him down. I walked around the next few days like a man condemned to the gallows. I kept thinking: *My witness for Christ is totally blown, and now my future plans are destroyed. Now what I am I going to do?* When my Christian friend Todd came to pick me up for Wednesday night Bible study, he could see how dejected I was.

"What's wrong bro?" Todd asked.

"I blew it; I got into a fight with my sister's boyfriend, and sinned against God."

As we sat in his car in my driveway, Todd explained to me that Jesus died so that we can be forgiven of our sin when we blow it. He also explained that nobody can deserve or earn forgiveness, and that it is a gift offered by God, and paid for by Jesus' blood when He sacrificed Himself on the cross. He had to explain it to me a couple of times for it to stick, but when I got it, a light came back on in my spirit. Then I realized, *I can't earn this! I can only accept it as a gift! You don't earn a gift, you accept a gift!* This single truth changed my life! I returned to God and received His grace. I was forgiven. God loved me and, once again, I knew it! This was a big step for me, and would have an impact on the direction that my life would take from that point on. However, I was still struggling with questions about my purpose, and what I would do with my life. *What now?* I knew that I needed something else. I needed a back-up plan.

CHAPTER 5

Contingency Plan

MY ASPIRATIONS FOR A CAREER in law enforcement had been ripped away. Once again, I was feeling lost and directionless. I battled depression and a sense of failure. I tried to keep myself busy to avoid idleness and boredom, my two worst enemies. I had too much idle time. I began to beat myself up for sabotaging my own future. *How could I have been so stupid?* I knew that I needed direction. I needed a contingency plan. I needed a "plan B." I attended church and continued to think long and hard about what my TIs had told me back at the academy. *You need more life experience.* I wondered. *How can I get more life experience? Life experience is all well and good, but I need something more immediate. I can't just wait around for some "life experience" to suddenly happen to me.*

Having completed the reserve police academy, I now focused more on my faith and God's purpose for my life. I remained zealous for my faith. I even started to reason that maybe God didn't want me to be a police officer. I knew that I wanted to serve God, and that gave me some sense of meaning. I determined that I would live my whole life serving Him.

One day, I was walking by the recruiters' offices near a strip mall near our bowling alley. I had seen them around. Army, Navy, Air Force, and Marines were listed on the front glass windows of the recruiters' offices, but I had never given it much thought. As the recruiters were standing in front of their offices, I stopped and talked to them for awhile. I went in and talked to each of the different branches. I wanted a clear picture of what all the jobs and the options were. I began thinking about joining the military, and how that could work together with God's plan for my life. The more I thought about it, the more excited I became. *This could be the contingency plan I've been looking for!*

Missions were being discussed that week at church, and I knew we had Marines in Beirut, Lebanon. That's when I thought of the military as a possible missions opportunity. Then it hit me. *This would give me the life experience that I needed! It would also give me direction and a source of income and independence. Moreover, it would look good later on my resume.* My consideration for which branch to join was hardly a debate. I would enlist in the United States Marine Corps. They were always extremely fit and looked sharp. Of all the branches of the military, the Marines made the greatest impression on me. They seemed set apart from all the other branches of service.

It was 1983, and the battle of Beirut, Lebanon, was going on at the time. I began to think, *who needs Jesus more than the Marines in Beirut?* I figured it would be a worthwhile mission, so I talked to my recruiter, a local gunny sergeant named John. The gunny was about six foot four inches tall and had a shaved head. He seemed like a nice guy. When he asked me what I wanted to do in the Marines, I told him without hesitation that I want to go into the infantry. He told me with confidence that that could be arranged. I took the ASVB (Armed Services Vocational Battery), signed the papers, and I was on my way.

As funny as it may sound, I sincerely wanted to serve Jesus in the Marine Corps. Later, upon careful reflection, I realized that there were other reasons I joined. The first, of course, was to serve God. The second reason was that I knew it would give me some much-needed life experience. Thirdly, and truth be told, I wanted to join for my independence. I was really looking for escape from all the pain and disappointment I associated with home. Enlisting seemed like a win-win. There was no apparent down side. I would get a job, a sense of respect, and sense of direction all in one fell swoop!

Marine Corps boot camp was twelve weeks of intensive training. I was on the delayed entry program and started boot camp on the fourteenth of November, 1983. I was taken to MCRD (Marine Corps Recruit Depot) in San Diego. When I arrived, they confiscated any personal belongings, issued our uniforms, and shaved our heads. I started just before Christmas. In the Corps, Christmas was treated like just another day, so when the holiday came around, I was a little surprised that it wasn't acknowledged. That night in my rack, I felt utterly alone as if I were a million miles away from home. I missed my family and friends terribly, and I quietly wept under my blankets. I wondered what had I gotten myself into? For the next twelve weeks we drilled, marched, worked out, and trained. We learned to take apart an M-16 rifle and put it back together in our sleep. They taught us the fine arts of marksmanship and hand-to-hand combat. We hiked many hills, training at Camp Pendleton. Some of these marches were particularly challenging. For example, on one night march during a storm, it was raining so hard that at one point, near the foot of a mountain, we sank in the mud way past the tops of our boots. The suction created by the mud anchored us to the ground in such a way that it required two other men to pull us out.

After graduating from boot camp, I was sent to Camp Pendleton for I.T.S. (Infantry Training School). There they taught us tactical warfare, how to use the LAAW (Light Anti-Tank Assault Weapon), the SAW (Small Automatic Weapon), and the M2O3 Grenade Launcher. We were taught hand-to-hand combat and were given bayonet training. We also learned how to use and rig claymore mines and how to use various other weapons. To me, all this was merely a means to an end. I was there to win Marines to Christ and to get as many saved as possible. It wasn't long before I finished I.T.S.

I received orders following I.T.S. to serve two years of barracks duty at Naval Weapons Station, Yorktown, Virginia.

After spending a week at home, I flew out to my new duty station not knowing what to expect. When I finally arrived, I was picked up with three other Marines at Norfolk Airport by a corporal. After loading our duffels into an olive green van, we were taken to Yorktown Naval Weapons Station. We arrived an hour later. I could see that this duty station was out in the middle of nowhere. Pine trees peppered the place as far as the eye could see. A compound of several thousand acres, this weapons station featured a high, chain-link fence with the customary razor wire around its perimeter. There was one gate in and out with a guard shack manned by an armed lance corporal. The Marines on staff there were as unwelcoming as the base was uninviting. I came in new with three others. As the newbies, we were treated like second-class citizens. Actually *worse!* None of us had a car or any form of transportation, and it was more than a thirty minute drive to any significant town. This underscored our sense of isolation.

The only activity was patrolling the dark, narrow roads of the base and checking bunkers during our night shift. The area was fraught with stories and legends. On the far end of the base was an old, dilapidated, two-story plantation house from the colonial period. The house was barely visible through the tree line. Its gray, peeling exterior and dark broken window panes gave it a creepy, haunted look. The story circulating was that the house once belonged to General Lee. Toward the end of the war, his daughter was supposedly captured and beheaded by union soldiers. According to Yorktown lore, at night the young woman could be seen on occasion walking headless in the woods near the old estate, her white gown prominent against the backdrop of the dark forest. That was only one of the many yarns spun by the Marines on base.

During my first year there, I hitched a ride a few times out to Virginia Beach. Being from the Huntington Beach area in California, I liked Virginia Beach. A small, quaint, beach community, much of it reminded me of home. Several of us agreed to split the cost of a hotel room. We were going to see the town, mingle with the locals, and meet back at the hotel room later. A problem soon arose when I realized that two of the guys (one of whom drove us there) intended to bring women back to the hotel room for the night. Apparently, they didn't mind sharing the space! That night I tried unsuccessfully to sleep. My buddies "consummating" with their new found girlfriends made sleeping impossible. I decided to get up and go for a walk. It was eleven o'clock, and Virginia Beach rolls up their sidewalks at eight. It was a ghost town. So I walked the streets with my backpack until I started to get tired. When my eyes got heavy, I looked for a place to bed down for the night. I found a church that was closed for the night. I donned a very large beach towel and, using my pack for a pillow, I slept in the alcove of the church's front porch. It served to keep the wind off me, and it was reasonably comfortable during the summer months.

I was up early on Sunday morning before anyone arrived at the church. I decided to attend the service. I found a local diner and used their restroom facilities to wash and clean up. The church was a large, traditional, red brick building with white trim and a steeple. I discovered that it was a Methodist church, and everyone was very warm and friendly. There I met a family whose last name was Vester. They were gracious and had a very cute daughter. They later invited me home for lunch. On the way to their home, Mrs. Vester was making conversation and trying to get to know me a little better when she suddenly asked me where I had stayed last night. The question caught me off guard. I didn't want to lie, but I didn't want to tell her that I had just spent last night sleeping on the street either. I fumbled for an answer. I told her that I worked a graveyard shift back at the base, and that I'm so used to being awake at that hour, that I couldn't sleep, and that I just spent the evening walking around seeing the town. I thought that it was a fairly good story, but I think that she saw through it. The family just took me in. They had me stay for dinner, and Mrs. Vester put pillows and blankets on the couch and encouraged me to get some rest. I fell fast asleep, only to wake up a couple of hours later fully rested. The Vesters showed me extraordinary kindness. They didn't even know me, and they treated me like one of their own. I have never forgotten them. I realized that God loved me through them at a time when I really needed it. I met up with the guys later that evening, and we drove back to the base.

After my first year at the Weapons Station, I knew that I didn't want to be there. The atmosphere in the barracks and among the Marines was dark and oppressive. Morale was low. Any sign of joy was immediately snuffed out by the established leaders of the unit. The personnel were unfriendly and distant. Nobody wanted to hear anything about God. The work environment was hostile and even abusive. For example, a common practice involved the more seasoned members of the guard taking each of the new members into the barracks where they would receive a beating or what some would call a *jumping in*. The new guy would come out all beaten up. For reasons that I can't explain, I was overlooked. I was never jumped in. Nevertheless, it was still the longest year of my life to date. It wasn't prison, but it seemed similar. The culture and mindset among the Marines on that base were very adolescent and prison-like. Worse yet, I had another long year ahead of me since it was a two-year assignment.

I decided that, if possible, I would transfer out. Any place else had to be better than this place. I made a request to see my staff sergeant. The staff sergeant had a high and tight haircut. He was a very short man with a very big ego, and had what I call "The Napoleon Syndrome." He talked with a New Jersey lisp, and he didn't like me from the get-go.

When I finally knocked on the doorway to his office, he asked, "What do you want Jacquesh?"

I said, "I would like to request a transfer to Camp Pendleton, Staff Sergeant."

"Jacquesh, do you weawy think the Mawine Corwps is going to give you a twansfer just because you want one? You'wre not going to get any twansfer, Jacquesh!"

"Well, Staff Sergeant, I would like to submit a written request anyway," I said.

The Staff Sergeant retorted, "Herew, filw dis owt!" he said, throwing the paperwork at me.

After filling it out, I returned my paperwork to him, seriously doubting that he would send it on to the next concerned party. Then I saw the staff sergeant place the request form on the corner of his desk in a black metal tray. I turned and left.

Not content with just leaving my request in the staff sergeant's hands, I hiked out to a very secluded place in the woods and poured my heart out to God. I pleaded with God, telling Him how much I wanted to go back to California. I knew that my request was not likely to be granted. If they did send me to the fleet, it would most likely be to the 2nd Marine Division in Camp Lejeune, North Carolina. This would be closer and less cost to the Federal Government. My request was for the 1st Marine Division on the opposite end of the country. After pleading my case before God, I waited.

Three weeks later, I was called to report to the staff sergeant's office. I thought that I was in trouble for something because three weeks would hardly be enough time to get a reply back regarding my transfer request. I thought, *No, it's too soon.*

When I came into the office, the staff sergeant said, "Jacquesh, I don't know how you got twansfered ov'r dare, but you've got owrd'rs to go weport to Camp Pend-w-ton. Herew! Take them and get ou'd a herew!"

As I took my orders from the staff sergeant, I glanced at the metal tray on his desk. There sat my transfer request. I thought that he had to have faxed my request, but even still, I knew the chances of my request being granted were almost nil. The more I thought about it, the more I was convinced. My transfer was a complete act of God and a whole year short of my original assignment! That was the only possible explanation in my mind. God had heard my desperate cry for help, and He had answered by delivering me from a very dark place. This increased my faith significantly. I had that glimmer of hope once again that God was in my life and that I was not alone. However, some of the greatest challenges I would ever face were looming on the horizon, waiting for me in California.

CHAPTER 6

Paper Tiger

A WEEK LATER, I WAS on a jet bound for LAX! There I was picked up with some other transfers and taken to a waiting station on Camp Pendleton. Then a bus arrived to pick me up and take me to my permanent post. My permanent post turned out to be Camp Horno. There, I was assigned to Lima Company, Third Battalion, 1st Marines, 2nd Platoon. I was a little out-of-sorts because I didn't know anyone and moving to a new assignment tends to be isolating. However, it didn't take long before I was meeting the guys I would spend the next three years of my life with. As I began to meet the men in 2nd platoon, I couldn't help but be struck by how unique each Marine was. With all the emphasis on uniformity in the Corps, these guys all shined with their own individual personalities. There was Lance Corporal Verhage, an all-state wrestler from Missouri and built like a fire plug. Verhage was a good-natured, gregarious fellow whose arms were as big as his legs. I would see him on more than one occasion pick up guys twice his size over his head and shake them, all in fun. There was also Lance Corporal Knops from Wisconsin who couldn't be serious even if his life depended on it. Always ready with a wisecrack or a joke, Knops kept everyone in stiches most of the time, and became our main source of comic relief. Lance Corporal Stallings was also quite an amusing fellow with his deep Southern accent. Then there was Lance Corporal Penske who had somewhat of a withdrawn and dark personality. There were many others whose names I can't remember. However, the three guys whose names would be indelibly written on my memory were Corporal

Tim Jones, Lance Corporal Bob Domecq, and Lance Corporal John Curtis.

These three men were all Christians, and when I met them we soon became fast friends. Corporal Jones often led our Bible studies and always had a word of encouragement and exhortation. These guys were serious about their faith, and we became brothers in the truest sense of the word. They would share very deeply from their hearts and were some of the most honest and transparent men I had ever known. Without hesitation, they prayed fervently for me and for each other when we went through dark and uncertain times in the Corps. We even attended church together at times when we had liberty. I thrived in the fleet. The brotherhood and the camaraderie were unparalleled. Life with my brothers was a true adventure with a shared sense of mission, and I advanced in my faith.

My Marine brothers struggled with deeper issues of the heart. They'd confessed their sins, sharing their pain and struggles with each other. In fact, they shared on a much deeper level than I did. As they did this, they offered counsel, support, and prayer for one another. Strangely, I never seemed to be plagued with the same struggles that they were dealing with. *I thought.* Corporal Jones and Lance Corporal John Curtis insisted that I had a lot of pain I was not dealing with, but I thought they were wrong. I thought that they were just missing it and were off base. As far as I was concerned, I had never been happier. Nothing seemed to faze me. I was impervious to insult and injury. I took everything in stride and with a smile. Moreover, all I seemed to be experiencing was the joy of the Lord! I wasn't being disingenuous or fake. I really did feel joyful most of the time.

I didn't realize that I was in a very special grace period. I was in a place where God was insulating me from all my past pain. I was still in my honeymoon phase with God, and I was not aware that I had unconsciously taken on my Christianity as another role. Having played different roles all my life, I put on my faith the same way, like another change of clothes. I knew what I thought a Christian was supposed to be, so I set out to be the *perfect Christian*. The result was what I call "Disneyland Christianity." Like a paper tiger, I had the persona and behavior of a good Christian without the authenticity and personal transformation. In other words, I was paper mache'-perfect on the outside without anything supporting my false persona on the inside. I had no true understanding of who I was. My identity was a fabrication, and I didn't know it.

I would later read about another disciple of Jesus, Peter, who was also a paper tiger before the Lord really got hold of him. Peter was convinced that he would even be willing to die for his Lord, even to the point that when the mob came for Jesus, Peter drew a sword cutting off the servant's ear. However, when Jesus insisted that he put down the sword, Peter lost courage. Peter had put his trust and his strength in exterior things, and when those things were removed he had nothing inside to support his convictions. So, he caved in during a crisis.

I was absolutely saved, and I had the Holy Spirit, but I had locked away my pain. I was completely out of touch with my true emotions. My pain was buried, so much so I was sincerely unaware that anything was wrong with me. My facade was a false identity. It was a veneer, a shell protecting my vulnerable, hurting, true self. However, I knew nothing of this, so I continued to live oblivious to my true emotions that were so deeply locked away. I was, in fact, a paper tiger. I think it bothered my Marine brothers that I was so out-of-touch with my personal pain. Even so, both God and my brothers were very gracious and patient with me.

We had a colonel over our battalion who was relatively laid back in his leadership style. What this meant for us was that our days were basically 6am to 5pm, with weekends and nights off. It was a great time, and I spent my liberty looking for a church in town. I soon began attending a church in Oceanside near the base. The church was called Twin Cities Christian Church. They had a great youth pastor who had all the young people fired up about their faith. It was a warm fellowship in a very charming, chapel-style, church building, but the best thing about it was that some very cute girls attended there. Being a young Marine and in the zenith of my youth, I had my pick. The girls seemed to fuss over me, and I loved the attention that I was getting there. I made many friends. We often spent our summer nights at the beach watching the sunset and singing songs around a fire pit. I loved the smell of the salt air and burning firewood. There was a very special kinship among the people in this group. The soft summer breeze and the warm feel of the sand against my feet served to imprint the moments I spent with these amazing people. The relationship and deep sense of connection I felt was profound. I thought, *this is heaven on earth*. I had never been happier. I even took some annual leave time to go on a church retreat for a week with my new church family.

I attended church there for the next three years any time I could. It was during this period that one girl began to stand out from all the rest, and I soon became smitten with a young woman named Tamba. She was deep, reflective, and godly. A strong woman of faith, She always gave me the impression that there was more going on behind her eyes than she was revealing. Often, she would pause for a moment, and tilt her head slightly before making a comment or answering a question. She had strawberry blond hair that was redder than blond, a curvaceous, attractive figure, and the most unusual, stunning, light-green eyes. Her cat-like features riveted my attention. She was eighteen, and yet seemed intelligent and wise beyond her years. On more than one occasion, she would surprise me with an insight or a question that seemed to emanate from someone much older. Moreover, she had a mutual interest in *me*. Our friendship grew, and it wasn't long before we began seeing each other on a regular basis. I was approaching my fourth year in the Marine Corps, and we soon fell fast in love.

It was 1987 when we started dating. However, our dating was cut short because Third Battalion, 1st Marines, was called up to police the Pacific rim, or what some call the *ring of fire*. This name refers to all the volcanic activity throughout the Pacific region. Marines refer to this tour as a WESTPAC. We would be spending the next six months on a ship patrolling the South Pacific. That wasn't the only change in store for us. We were all informed that our battalion would have a new colonel. This colonel, as it turned out, was not so laid back. As a matter of fact, this colonel was the exact opposite of his predecessor. This guy was tough, and he volunteered our battalion for every possible training operation there was. All the Marines referred to him as "Colonel Dark Side." He was given this name because any time he addressed the battalion over the speaker system, he spoke in this deep, resonant voice that resembled Darth Vader.

It wasn't long before we were underway and heading to the islands of Alaska. We took an LHA3, what was essentially a small aircraft carrier. The LHA3 was primarily designed for Harriers, Helios, and troop transport. When we got into the Northern Alaskan waters our ship, as big as it was, was bobbing like a cork in the water. Men everywhere were losing their lunches. The berthing areas were filled with the foul smells of vomit as both Marines and Sailors alike sought to gain their sea legs. We finally began to turn south toward Korea and made a stop in Pusan where we trained with the ROK (Republic of Korea) Marines. The ROK Marines were impressive and disciplined soldiers.

Moreover, the Korean people were hospitable and friendly. Tim, Bob, John, and I spent most of our liberty walking around Seoul and Pusan visiting the coffee shops and the local bathhouses. The bathhouses were interesting because they all had at least three pools of differing temperatures. One pool was freezing cold while another would be more moderate, and still another was so hot you could barely stand it! We would stay in the cold pool until we couldn't stand it anymore, then we would all get out and jump in the steaming hot pool. It gave us quite a head rush. Foolish I know, but when you are a young Marine you think you are indestructible.

Tamba and I were missing each other terribly and writing to each other often. The problem with long distance relationships is that it becomes very easy to idealize each other. By not spending any real time together it becomes easy to paint the perfect fantasy. This idealizing worked mostly to my advantage since she was, most definitely, the genuine article. Over the next six months I continued to write to Tamba sending postcards and letters. My goal was to write her from every port. Then I got this great idea! I would send her a message in the form of a scrabble! By doing this I would let her figure out the message over the course of the next several months. I eventually acquired postcards from every country we stopped at. So, I took a black marker and wrote one big capital letter on the back of each postcard from all the various ports. Some were from Korea, Singapore, Okinawa, Japan, Thailand, Philippines, and Australia. I then lined up all the postcards, and wrote out my message with each postcard having only one character. Then I scrambled them and mixed them all up. After collecting them together, I sent only two or three at a time, randomly, two weeks apart. After receiving the last of the postcards, Tamba would find they spelled out, "I'M IN LOVE WITH TAMBA DAVISON!" We continued to write, growing in love as we learned more about each other through our letters. And though our love was immature, it was very real nonetheless.

As much as I was missing Tamba, I was really enjoying my time overseas. Corporal Tim Jones led Bible studies for our small group of Christians. We became a very tight circle, always encouraging others to join. Once, a Christian brother, who was a Navy SEAL, wanted to join us. I think he was attracted to the kinship we shared as a group. For a while he was hanging out with us when we would get into port, but his team discouraged him from associating with us, so he stopped. Over time we began to win other Marines to Christ. Some of the guys in Weapons Platoon were not happy about this at all, and vented their hostility often in the form of the most popular expletives.

Our faith in Jesus brought us into conflict more than once on ship. One time after leaving a port, I came into the berthing area (sleeping quarters) to find some of the Marines watching pornography on the VCR. The volume was turned up loud. Moreover, some of those who were new in the faith were getting drawn in. I just couldn't stand by and say nothing because I felt responsible for those we had been leading to Christ, so I stood in front of the TV screen, faced everyone and said, "How can you guys turn your backs on God like this?" I continued to repeat myself. Guys from Weapons Platoon began to curse and swear. "JACQUES GET THE $#%&* OUT OF HERE!" Boots were hurled at me that I quickly deflected. It was well worth it though, because two of our new believers got up and walked out. Later, Corporal Jones filed a formal complaint to our command with the result that an order was issued that pornography was no longer allowed to be viewed on ship. This obviously did not make us very popular with some, least of all Weapons Platoon.

On another occasion when we were crossing the equator, the Navy began to implement their traditional Shellback initiation for all the new Sailors and Marines. The tradition goes back years. Before, a new Sailor or Marine has crossed the equator they are considered to be what they call a "Wog," a derogatory term for a greenhorn or newbie. It's only after passing over the equator and going through the Shellback initiation that a person could claim the proud title of "Shellback." For this initiation, the deck of the ship is turned into somewhat of an obstacle course requiring new Sailors and Marines to go through this gauntlet of garbage, old food dumped on deck, and other forms of hazing. It's a humiliating display of subjugation. Initiates are required to crawl on their bellies from one end of the ship to the other only to finally reach the end where they are forced to bow down and pay homage to "King Neptune," one of the ship crew dressed in a toga, and kiss his feet. And not just his feet, but also the feet of his queen (a guy dressed in drag). For us as Christians, we understood King Neptune to be a pagan god. Therefore, we could not, in good conscience, participate in this pagan ritual. We could only bow down and serve the true and living God. Our objections were met with ridicule, but in the end, we were restricted to the berthing area while the initiation ceremony was underway. No harm, no foul.

The Marine Corps was always a big test for new believers. Numerous times when coming into port, many of the servicemen would go into town and spend most of their hard-earned money on booze and prostitutes. It wasn't uncommon for Marines to come back to the ship in a drunken stupor, and wake up the next morning with tattoos, black eyes, and an occasional disease they didn't remember getting.

Tim Jones, Bob Domeq, John Curtis, and I would spend our liberty exploring whatever country we found ourselves in, seeking out the local missionaries and visiting churches. The wonderful thing was that we always found a connection and a mutual kinship among the believers of other nations. We were always well received and treated like family. Moreover, we were often given inside information about restaurants and places to stay, as well as places to avoid by our indigenous brothers and sisters. In countries like Korea, Thailand, Philippines, and Australia we were often shown amazing hospitality by the local believers. For example, in Australia our Christian brothers and sisters in Sydney gave us lodging for the night and took us around town the next day. They took us to the Blue Mountains where we were brought to the edge of a sheer cliff face. Just beneath us was what looked like a carpet of clouds at our feet. It looked as if you could just step out and walk on them. Later, they took us to some caverns that were absolutely spectacular! Australia was an amazing place with beaches that reminded me of California. It was one of those few places that I didn't want to leave.

After saying goodbye to our local brothers and sisters, we were shipping out and heading toward Hawaii where we docked at Pearl Harbor in Oahu. We were all given 24 hours of liberty before shipping out the next day. My buddies and I had never been to Hawaii, and we wanted to make the most of the opportunity, so we decided to head for the beach. The water was a beautiful aqua blue and bathtub warm. The area where we were swimming was enclosed by a very large jetty. As we looked out, we could see the waves breaking over the top of the rocks. We all decided that it would be fun to swim out to the jetty and climb up on the rocks. Being Marines, everything was a competition; we raced to see who could get out there first. When we got to the jetty, we found that it was made of very rough and sharp lava rock. We were careful about climbing up to the top of the jetty, but not carful enough to avoid getting blown off the top by a monster wave. John fell backwards, ripping the skin off half his back. Bob was sliced with two large gashes in his shoulder. I landed on my feet resulting in some very deep cuts on the bottoms of my feet. We were all hurting and shaken. There we were, treading water, and bleeding from various parts of our bodies.

We slowly started to make our way to shore, the salt water adding a stinging insult to our injuries. When we finally got to shore, I realized that I would have to walk across the hot sand with open cuts on my feet. Not good. We stopped, sat down, and began to assess our situation as blood continued to run from our cuts and abrasions. All of us knew that going back to the ship was not an option. In our current condition, once back on ship the ship's crew would never allow us to go ashore again. After a brief conference, we determined that our only option was to find a local drug store in Waikiki, buy the necessary medical supplies, and patch ourselves up. Then we could at least hobble around town for the rest of the night. We looked ridiculous. Nonetheless, there was no way we were going to miss out on our only day in Hawaii.

Besides our determination not to miss out on Hawaii, we knew we would be heading home soon afterwards. This would be our last whoo-ha! It proved to be a great time in spite of our injuries. The day was over before we knew it, and we were back on ship. When our ship left port, there was energy and excitement as we were all anticipating our last trek back to California. We were finally heading home!

================ CHAPTER 7 ================

Operation Marathon

Marathon: a test of endurance. Typically a 26 mile run designed to test a person's physical and mental toughness.

AFTER SIX MONTHS AT SEA, we were finally all healed up and back in California! I couldn't wait to see Tamba. I was missing her badly, thinking about her every day while away. I was on pins and needles anticipating our reunion. I was so looking forward to spending time with her that I could barely stand it. Then it happened. Circumstances took an unexpected turn. Unbeknownst to us, we were about to embark on Operation Marathon. At Pendleton, we learned that Colonel Dark Side had scheduled 3/1 (Third Battalion-First Marines) for a whole series of training operations. It had been predetermined. Being part of the rank and file infantry division meant that we were the last to hear about our next expeditionary mission. After six months overseas we were all ready for some down time and a little R&R. However, that wasn't going to happen, because 3/1 was scheduled to hit the ground running. This meant no liberty. We were told that we would be getting on buses at zero dark thirty the next morning and heading out to Mountain Warfare Training School, Bridgeport, California, in the Northern Sierras for two weeks of cold weather survival training. That night we were issued cold weather gear. This included a parka, snow shoes, and a mountain pack that held sixty more pounds of supplemental gear. We flew out the following day and landed on a base in northern California. There we were picked up by buses and shuttled out to Bridgeport.

At our destination we spent our first night in a yurt. This is nothing more than a wooden structure with a canvas covering like a tent. Our instructor's name was Sergeant Mayo. Lance Corporal Knopps couldn't leave that alone, always referring to the instructor as "Sergeant Mayo- naise," He would stretch out the name as he said it. Knopps wore out that name quick time. Our training for the following two weeks involved learning how to ski with 60 pounds on our backs. This would include an M-16 rifle, a utility harness with ammunition pouches, canteens, magazines, and a bayonet. Not exactly a resort experience!

We were required to dig a snow cave and sleep in it, which proved to be a challenging experience. We did this during a whiteout or blizzard conditions. We were cold and wet most of the time. We were instructed to carve out shelvings in our snow caves. On these we would roll out our ice support mats and sleeping bags and try to sleep. The caves were heated and illuminated by nothing more than candles. Try sleeping in an icebox, and you'll have some idea what this is like. The goal was not comfort, but survival in harsh blizzard conditions. Trying to sleep was another challenge. The candles combined with our own body heat would cause the ceiling to crack. As the night wore on, the crack in the ceiling got wider and wider. Consequently, more than a few of us had to be dug out of a collapsed snow cave. To say that we were miserably cold would be an understatement. There were Marines who actually came home with some mild forms of frostbite. After two weeks in the snow, it finally came to an end. I think those were the longest two weeks of my life.

The buses then took us to a nearby airport where we were flown to the desert. We landed in Twenty-Nine Palms for desert warfare training. It was very hot, dusty, and windy when we arrived, but we weren't complaining; we were just glad to be out of the cold. The temperature was between 98 and 105 degrees, closer to what we were used to. But hey...at least it was dry heat! My whole company stayed in a very large common tent filled with rows of cots. We were trained in weapons used to pierce armored vehicles and to bust open enemy bunkers and other fortifications. After completing a large training operation involving the whole battalion, we were given orders to pack up. The following morning we staged our gear in rows on the ground. Once we had the buses packed up, we were told that we were flying to Panama for jungle warfare training school.

We were all looking at each other, wondering when we would get a chance to see home again. The most difficult thing was not the training, but not having any known timeline. We could handle almost anything, but the unknown was the most challenging. Having no reference point or timeline was much more difficult and psychologically challenging. Apparently, the command didn't think we needed to know when we were going home. The only thing we knew was that we were the only battalion doing nonstop operations. We got to the airport, and an hour later 3/1 was on a number of C-130s (what they call a Hirky Bird) flying to Panama. The C-130 is a cargo transport plane. Let me tell you that they are not built for comfort. This aircraft was built strictly for utilitarian purposes. It's noisy, and there is no climate control so it gets very cold at high altitude. We should have brought earplugs, but for most of us this was our first rodeo. Consequently, our ears were ringing hours after we stepped off the plane. We landed at Fort Davis, an army base. There we would be briefed and trained by the army rangers stationed there. After being assigned sleeping quarters and issued our jungle gear, we were taken to a large room for briefing. There the instructors informed us of all the things in the jungle that could kill us or at least be detrimental to our health: what's poisonous, what bites, what you should try to avoid, and where we could find drinkable water. After the briefing, I thought to myself, *it can't be that dangerous. They're just trying to scare us.* Once again, I was wrong.

As a kid, I was always fascinated with wild life, and to my mom's dismay I always had a continual stream of different creatures kept in cages and tanks in my bedroom. Anything I could catch or buy locally became a pet. This included ants, potato bugs, crickets, lizards, snakes, a gopher, rats, fish, and a crayfish. When my fish started to disappear, I got rid of the crayfish. My dad once bought me a tarantula for my birthday. It was the biggest spider I'd ever seen! It was a perfect addition to the rest of my exotic collection which included a love bird given to me by a friend. For a while I also kept an iguana acquired at the local pet shop. All in all, my parents were fairly supportive of my interests. This fascination with animals allowed me to create my own world and allowed me to escape some of the harsher realities that I was dealing with at the time.

Now here I was, at the age of twenty-three in Panama, about to go into the jungle, a *real* jungle! A jungle like the ones I had always watched on National Geographic! I couldn't wait, and my excitement energized me. I knew this would be the experience of a lifetime.

The jungle was dark with a very thick canopy above us that virtually blocked-out the daylight. A dank smell of dead leaves accompanied a hot, wet drizzle. My excitement was soon mitigated by the Marine Corps' main objective: Jungle Warfare Training. Our training involved sleep deprivation and learning to survive in jungle conditions. We did this while navigating through miles of jungle terrain every day. This required us to cross large, wide, green rivers with our gear intact. Given our setting, we were most concerned about crocodiles and piranha. We all told each other that the Marine Corps would not put us in that kind of jeopardy under training conditions, but no one seemed convinced. We crossed the river in pairs. By the luck of the draw, the guy I was paired with couldn't swim. He was afraid of the water. But who could blame him given the circumstances. I was always a strong swimmer, having grown up with a large swimming pool, and having spent most of my summers body-boarding at Huntington Beach. My swimming buddy just hung on to our gear while I did a breast stroke dragging him behind me with one hand seeking the river's edge. The river's edge was somewhat deceptive because of all the overhang from trees along the shoreline. Just when you thought you were across, you discovered that you were just entering the overhang. Then you had to maneuver around many plants before actually touching mud. Another challenge was locating your fellow Marines on the other side of the riverbank because the strong current had pulled us way downstream. Consequently, we didn't end up on the direct opposite bank. Fighting the strong currents, we all found ourselves way down stream. Once on the other side, we had to navigate through thick, dense vegetation to locate and reconnect with the rest of our squad.

Once we all arrived on the other side of the river, our squad reassembled. Then we resumed blazing a trail through the jungle using a machete. We continued moving through heavy vegetation, much of which was impassable. This required our squad to snake its way through the jungle, taking detours and reconfiguring our compass settings when necessary. We continued this practice until we came to a sheer cliff with a heavy waterfall plummeting down about two-hundred feet. This made it imperative to rapel off this cliff down to the jungle floor. The experience was amazing. By the time we all got down to the bottom, it became obvious that we were not going to get back to our barracks before nightfall. This meant that we would be sleeping in the jungle overnight. Not good. This is something you want to avoid if possible. What made this prospect *interesting* was that the jungle floor literally comes alive at night with every kind of life form imaginable. The challenge was trying to sleep on the jungle floor without getting bitten or stung. We had been taught to run a line between two trees so we could drape our rain poncho over the line. Then by cutting two thin branches we could create a shelter that would balance over the line and protect us from the rain. We then could tie our mosquito net underneath to the sticks holding out the poncho. A person could avoid getting bitten by draping the net over them and by tucking it underneath a very thin polypropylene blanket. This would keep the myriad of insects and animals out of your immediate sleeping area.

The days were long. The rain and the drizzle were practically non-stop, and we were continually wet. Sleep was practically nonexistent. I figured that we were probably averaging between one and a half to two hours of sleep per day, this after the most physically demanding and intensive training on the planet. Even so, I was actually enthralled by the jungle. The calls of small howler monkeys in the trees, despite their size, sounded like King Kong. I saw ants that were two inches long, which is no exaggeration. They had to be as big as small mice. It was truly like "The Lost World." I found it all very interesting, but it kept bringing my thoughts back to why I was there. I realized that I was training for war, and that I might someday be required to face this element in wartime conditions with a real enemy, and that we would actually be trying to kill each other. It was a sobering thought.

On our third day of training operations, we were dropped again in the middle of the Panamanian jungle. It was very hot, and in these sauna-like conditions we remained soaking wet. The smell of compost in various stages of decomposition filled the air as we made our way through this rain forest. We had orders to determine our coordinates and navigate through the jungle all the way back to base camp. With very few provisions, and less than six hours of sleep in the last three days, we once again began to make our way through this hot, wet, jungle. We shot an azimuth with our compass and then started blazing a trail in a straight line back to base camp.

The jungles of Panama are thick, and the canopy is dense. The jungle is dark in the daytime and pitch black at night. Try taking a compass setting with a wall of vegetation in front of you, and you'll soon discover how difficult it is. Much of the time, we were taking compass settings on a fixed point, in this case a tree in front of us, usually just a few feet away, only to stop and take another. It was tedious and slow-going. Fatigue and sleep deprivation often made a person careless which is hazardous in this terrain. Everything either bites, stings, or sticks you in the jungle. We were warned about the fer-de-lance, aka, the two-step snake, as well as the bushmaster, larger than its cousin, another highly venomous snake. Both were known to have a combination of hemotoxic and neurotoxic venoms which attack the victim's bloodstream and the nervous system simultaneously. It became very obvious early on that if anyone got bitten, they would never be extracted in time. Later on in our expedition a Marine killed a fer-de-lance with the butt of his rifle. That put aside any illusions that it was just talk. Occasionally, we would see brightly colored, poison arrow frogs. The locals practiced tipping their blow-darts with the extremely toxic secretions from the animal's skin. Another hazard was bullet ants, known to inflict one of the most painful stings on the planet, ergo the name. They liked to hang out on tree trunks. This always kept us mindful of where we were placing our hands. Add to this a whole host of wasps, spiders, and hornets, all of which had equally aggressive dispositions. Vampire bats were also an issue, which is why we had to have a "bat watch" at night. The sentry would walk (or stumble) around for an hour at night with a flashlight making sure no bats would land and crawl up on us as we slept. After his hour was up, the next man would take his place, and these rounds continued until daybreak.

Another nemesis of equal concern was black palm. These were thin palm trees with brittle, barbarous, needle-like projections that would often break off in the skin if a person absent-mindedly grabbed onto a tree. The problem was that it was always raining in the jungle, and the jungle is very hilly, so between the hills and the rain, boots would collect mud and lose traction. When you're slipping, the natural thing to do is to steady yourself by gabbing hold of a tree. Needless to say, we brought home a lot of black palm.

So there we were, one squad of twelve men trying to blaze our way through this strange Jurassic environment. We had been given a machete to make a trail. The jungle was so dense that we could only travel in a single file. The point man would chop his way through the flora until his arm muscles were exhausted. Then he would hand the machete to the next guy in line and go to the back until it was his turn again. I was behind eight other guys when we all heard it, a scream reverberating through the jungle, like someone dying. Before I knew what was happening, a whole squad of Marines had been mowed over by the point man running to get away. He had chopped into a hive of Africanized killer bees. Our squad scrambled to get away. The bees assaulted our squad with vigorous fervor. They swarmed us with lightning speed, and we couldn't get away fast enough. We were all stung, some badly. I received nine stings, five on top of my head and four on my hand.

That wasn't the worst of it. We absolutely needed the machete which had been dropped right under the hive when Lance Corporal Meaks executed his enthusiastic getaway. Meaks was ordered to go back and retrieve the essential blade. He launched an emphatic protest, but only avoided another encounter with the hive because Lance Corporal Verhage said he would retrieve it. It was a valiant act by Lance Corporal Verhage. When we finally cleared the area, we tended our wounds. The stings on the top of my head began to throb and felt like open sores oozing blood. The pain was brilliant. That didn't matter. We were expected to ignore pain and keep going. We continued our march through the jungle. My head was pounding because of the bee stings. I thought about Tamba in brief and fleeting moments, almost too tired to think at all. I wondered where she was. I thought about the day and time and tried to imagine where she would be and what she might be doing. With a physically demanding schedule and very little sleep, we were all at the point of exhaustion. We eventually completed our training and, finally, after two weeks, it was over. When we completed the course we each received a certificate of completion. Hoorah!

I thought about Tamba often on the way back and wondered if I would get to see her. None of my fellow Marines knew if we were coming or going, literally. By this time, it seemed like one training op just bled into the very next one. Consequently, none of us knew if we were truly going back because we were never informed until the last minute. Though we were all being cautiously optimistic, we didn't get our hopes up. When we finally landed in San Diego, spirits were high. We could smell the ocean salt in the air, and we were looking forward to getting back and settled. The buses came and picked us up. We were heading up Interstate 5 toward Camp Pendleton! Home at last! Camp Pendleton was just within eye-shot when our buses suddenly turned into BUDS (Basic Underwater Demolitions School) at Coronado. This facility is where the Navy SEALS are trained and is right next to Pendleton, so we never saw it coming. We all just looked at each other like, *O-kay...here we go again!*

When we got there, we all filed off the buses and stood in formation. We were issued some tan shorts, and told that we were about to go through a water survival course. This involved treading water for 30 minutes. Then we were taken out and dropped into the deep ocean water. There we made a human circle with our arms interlinked as we floated together. This exercise was to increase the odds of survival in the event that your ship was sinking and you had to abandon ship with others in open water. After completing the exercise, we swam back. When we got to the beach we changed back into UDTs aka camouflage pants and t-shirts, and then were taken through a rigorous obstacle course that the SEALs call a confidence course. There we did a number of different exercises. Though we were exhausted to begin with, we made it through.

When all was said and done, they put us back on the bus, and we continued toward the main gate of Camp Pendleton. Pendleton is a very long military base, and it's a significant drive from one end to the other. On the north end of the base is the little town of San Clemente and on the other end is the city of Oceanside. The towns are about twenty-one and a half miles apart, and that's a straight line by freeway. When we got back from Coronado we came through the main gate, which is the Oceanside or south end of the base. Our camp was on the San Clemente side or the north end of the base, so when the buses stopped at the main gate and we were told to get out, I was a little suspicious. I was leery because I knew that it was over 20 miles to camp Horno, our base camp.

We all stepped warily off the bus and were ordered to stage our gear and get into formation. As we did this, the platoon sergeants began passing out small sack lunches in paper bags. I looked at my watch. It was twelve noon. I always knew the corps to be very scheduled, so I thought, *Well, the Marine Corps is very regimented about meals. We're just stopping to have lunch.* When I looked in my lunch bag I found one apple, a small carton of milk, and a baloney cheese sandwich. After finishing the contents therein, one of the sergeants shouted, "Saddle up!"

Now every Marine immediately knew what *saddle up* meant. We were going on a force march, which is a hike at a break-neck pace. My immediate thought was a question. *Where are we going? It certainly couldn't be Camp Horno!*

Yes! It was Camp Horno! It felt like the Bataan death march. Already physically spent from weeks of serial operations, we were now told to march over 20 miles across hills and mountains with our gear and rifles. It was a hot August afternoon and the temperature was in the high 90s. Our platoon commanders (usually second lieutenants) gave orders from Colonel Dark Side that any Marines who fell out of the march and didn't make it back would forfeit his liberty and get extra PT (physical training) for the rest of the week. When all our gear, packs, and rifles were on, the platoon sergeants yelled out, "Ready... March! Left, left, left, right left! My thighs began to burn as we started to bite into the grade of our first elevation gain. The sun blazed, unrelenting. The smell of sage and liquorice plants filled the air, and I drank it in. I loved that smell. Smelled like home to me. Even with the major challenge ahead of us, I was still encouraged to be going home.

We continued our march through the fierce August heat. Salt from our bodies stung our skin. Our faces baked under our helmets. With very little food and water for fuel, 3/1 hiked a force march all the way back to Horno up and down the mountains, hills, and valleys of Pendleton. In many of the valleys and ravines the temperature would spike like a furnace. The march proved to be more than many could endure. The colonel rode up front in a jeep. As you can guess, that didn't sit well with most of the guys. Some cursed under their breath as they saw the colonel bouncing up the dusty fire road. We all knew, of course, that this trek was to ultimately prepare us for the rigors of combat. War would never be easy on us, so neither would the colonel.

We were about seven miles into the march when the first men started to fall out. I was determined to make it all the way, compelled by the thought of seeing my girlfriend. There's nothing like love to motivate a serviceman. I settled into a mindless rhythm, listening to the drumming of boots on the march. It became a mechanical operation of body parts just doing what they do. I shut out everything else and just focused on the dusty trail in front of me. We marched on through the shimmering waves of heat coming off the hard, sunbaked landscape ahead of us. Eventually the trail would end, and I determined that I would be standing when it did. By the fifteenth mile mark, bodies were strewn everywhere to the right and left of the trail. Some suffered from heat exhaustion and needed to be picked up for medical attention. Finally, after over 20 miles of marching in the extreme heat we arrived back at our camp. When we arrived, we were told to shower and dress for chow time.

We had just finished one of the most rigorous and demanding training agendas any military unit could experience, and I came out victorious! What I didn't know was that the challenge that I had just endured would pale in comparison to what awaited me in the next few months.

CHAPTER 8

Shangri-La

I WAS ON TOP OF the world! I felt like I could do anything! I felt invincible, unstoppable and indestructible! I was numbered with the mighty! At 175 pounds, I was the strongest and in the best shape I'd ever been. That weekend, all those who finished the force march were rewarded with weekend liberty. I took immediate advantage of my favored status and caught the first bus into town to meet my girl. Tamba and her mother Cheryl picked me up at the bus stop. There she was, the girl I had waited so long to see. Tamba came bounding up and jumped into my arms with a squeal of excitement and a tight embrace. After a warm hug from Cheryl, we got in the car to drive to their house.

On the drive I noticed a quality about Tamba's mother, Cheryl. There was a dignity, wisdom, and an inner strength about her. Cheryl was a professional, statuesque woman. She was also very gracious, and invited me to stay the weekend. It was great to get off base and sleep in a real home for a change. I was allowed to sleep in the downstairs living room. After we had lunch, Tamba told me to go look in her bedroom upstairs. I immediately went upstairs. When I looked in, the aroma of cinnamon and scented candles met me right away. When I scanned Tamba's room, I noticed a lot of things one would expect to see in a young woman's bedroom: down pillows, a bedspread, a feminine-looking nightstand, lace drapes that filtered the sunlight streaming through the window, pictures and various other kinds of bric-a-brac. But when I looked up, there on the wall, I saw all the postcards I had sent to her strung together perfectly displaying my message: "I'M IN LOVE WITH TAMBA DAVISON!"

Later, Tamba and I went for a walk around her house. The house was an attractive, two-story, cottage-style home in suburbia. The yard was nicely landscaped with a number of potted plants, flowers, and trellises with an assortment of creeping vines. There were some fields nearby dotted by a number of eucalyptus trees. It was a clear, warm, summer day and the grass was tall. The day couldn't have been more perfect. A soft, warm breeze tickled our faces. I was intoxicated by love as the fragrance of eucalyptus, jasmine and honeysuckle mixed in the air. *This must be what heaven is like*, I thought.

As we continued walking, we came into a small copse of trees. She stopped. "This is it." She said. "This is my secret place. This is the place I come to when I want to be alone with God." I knew this place was special to her, and it seemed almost sacred. There was a pause, and for a moment everything seemed to stop. We gazed a long moment into each other's eyes. She held my gaze. Then I kissed her. We held each other for a long moment before returning to the house.

We talked and shared for hours that day. I knew that I loved this woman. Her beauty, depth and intelligence captivated me. This was heaven on earth, being with the woman I loved on a day like this. I couldn't imagine being happier or experiencing anything better. I was, for all intents and purposes, living a dream, and I felt a million miles away from my broken past.

When people think of a place with the most idyllic, utopian conditions, they will often use terms like Eden, Nirvana, or Shangri-La. It is a place that the human heart intuitively knows about, and many spend their whole lives searching for it. Many, maybe even most, never see it. I, on the other hand, was feeling it…seeing it… experiencing it. It was the same feeling I had had up in the mountains, with my Christian brothers and sisters at camp, or with my church group around the fire pit at the beach in Oceanside. It was a profound sense of connection with God and others. My explanation falls short of capturing the experience. It was the sense that I was highly valued and dearly loved. Maybe it was only for a brief moment; maybe it was just for a short season of time, but this much I do know. It was all very real. I thought, *This is too good to be true. I have never experienced so much happiness before.* I wanted it to last forever. This was my Shangri-La. It was an enchanted moment, and I feared breaking the spell.

Tamba and I saw each other often that summer and our relationship grew more intimate. That summer we attended a number of church functions and went to a Dennis Agajanian concert. I also went to watch her play volleyball with what looked like some very high level competitors. We spent as much time together as possible. On Sundays we would meet at church, and I would go home with her in a cobalt blue '68 Mustang. At the end of the weekend, she would drive me to catch the bus in Oceanside and head back to Camp Pendleton. We followed that pattern throughout the summer just before the fall when she would begin college.

It was during this time that I met Tamba's father. He and Cheryl had been divorced for a number of years, and he had settled in San Clemente. He was a distinguished, self-made man and very successful. He had started his own trucking company and was doing very well for himself. Tamba and I visited him one day. The visit was brief, and I got the distinct feeling that he didn't approve of his daughter dating a Marine. His tone and demeanor told me he didn't think that I was good enough for her. I didn't think that it was strange or unusual for a father to think that way. During that visit he mentioned that he wanted to buy Tamba a new car for college. This, of course, excited her.

After our visit, when Tamba and I got back to her house, she began discussing with her mother how they were going to sell the Mustang. I piped up and said, "I'll buy it!" They both turned and looked at me. "I like the car. It's clean-looking, runs well, and besides, I need a car." We made the transaction not long afterwards, and I became the proud owner of this cobalt blue, classic '68 Mustang.

I felt certain that I would eventually marry Tamba, but I wasn't giving it much thought at the time. I was very young in my thinking, and marriage seemed a long way off. I figured it would just take care of itself; that it would take its natural course.

One day as we were sharing, Tamba was showing me a book, a registry of sorts. It was a list of the names of all the top students in the nation who had graduated with high honors. As I scanned down the list, near the top of the D section was Tamba's name: "Davison, Tamba Bethany." I was amazed. This girl had maintained a perfect GPA throughout high school. I should have felt elation and pride for having such an intelligent and excellent girlfriend. That defining moment, however, revealed something in me that, up to that point, I was unaware of...it was fear.

Until then, as far as I knew, I was fearless. Nothing fazed me. I thought I had outgrown my fear. I thought I had left it back in my childhood, and it made me wonder briefly. I tried not to think much about it, shrugging off the feeling. Over time though, the fear kept coming back, haunting me like an old ghost. I kept trying to ignore it. Fear, however, was steadily growing, gaining a foothold again in my life. For the next few weeks I tried to pretend that things were normal with me. As time went on though, I realized more and more how very gifted Tamba really was. Not only was she a 4.0 student, but she was also a great athlete and excelled in volleyball. As we continued dating, that fear kept returning again and again. Each time seemed stronger than the last. Eventually, the fear became a continual anxiety that plagued me. I tried to understand it and analyze it, but it wasn't going away. I just kept thinking of how bright, beautiful, and gifted Tamba was, and what a worthless failure and loser I had been. I began comparing, a fatal mistake.

Up to this point, nothing had fazed me or bothered me. On duty, insult and injury bounced off me like a tennis ball off a Sherman Tank. I had an unwavering boldness and confidence that shined like the sun. But now, suddenly, it seemed that all my confidence had been sapped. It had somehow been drained away. On the outside, I had a rock-solid veneer; however, on the inside I was discovering a raging cauldron of fear and insecurity. I was unraveling inside and I couldn't understand why. I just kept entertaining this irrational fear that when Tamba discovered my troubled past, my failures, and dismal grade point average, that she would drop me like a child dropping a hot iron. I feared rejection, though I didn't realize it at the time. I actually feared abandonment, something that I had experienced time and time again as a child. Growing up, it wasn't uncommon for me to come home and find that my family was emotionally unavailable. At that moment, I didn't understand how my dysfunctional family life led to my overwhelming fear of rejection. I never gave it a second thought, and I wasn't making the connection at that moment.

Tamba loved me no doubt, and she had proved it in a number of ways. The fear, however, only continued to grow more intense as I continued to make comparisons. She was very popular with people and had lots of friends. Growing up, I had no real friends, certainly no one who admired me. Everyone I met thought very highly of Tamba. In contrast, it seemed that I had always been a big disappointment to my parents, teachers, and coaches. While Tamba was a great student athlete. I never thought I was very good in sports and for the most part lacked the interest. She was a 4.0 honor student while I had barely graduated from high school. As I continued to make these comparisons, I began to feel myself shrink inside. I was becoming smaller and smaller. I was becoming a non-entity.

My mental and emotional state deteriorated. This started to manifest itself in extreme passivity and manipulation, not very attractive qualities. I began trying to mitigate the fear by using the only coping strategies I had known growing up. I would placate and try to please everyone. I would be the perfect boyfriend, catering to her every whim, and I would deny myself. I would be, once again, playing a role, the very thing I had been accustomed to my whole life. However, placating didn't work in this situation. I became a non-entity in the relationship. Paranoid that I might make a mistake and be rejected, I remained silent in situations when the appropriate thing to do was to speak up. I was constantly deferring to Tamba without giving any input or expressing any opinion. I had now been a Christian for four years, and still had no sense of my own identity.

As my confidence disintegrated, our relationship started to change. My seeming lack of self-respect began to eat away at the respect in the relationship. Tamba would *test* me now and then, expecting me to put my foot down, draw a line in the sand. I think she was trying to find out if I still had a clear boundary, an opinion, a sense of self. Each time, however, I failed the test. My own immaturity and blindness kept me from being able to understand the relational dynamics that were in play. The strategies that had worked for me my whole life and enabled me to survive childhood were no longer working for me as a man. I sought to do anything to please her. My actions, however, came out of fear and a pathetic sense of desperation, and she could see it. Without respect there can be no love because respect is the foundation that love is built on. She was committed and patient with me, nonetheless. My Shangri-La was burning down as I started a rapid descent into the valley of the shadowlands.

CHAPTER 9

The Descent

MY DREAM WAS SUDDENLY BECOMING a nightmare. Tamba was just beginning her first semester at Pacific Christian College in Fullerton, California where she had signed up for the volleyball league. I was still in the Marine Corps and had three more months before receiving my honorable discharge. Tamba was now in Fullerton, a two hour drive north from Camp Pendleton. She had jumped into school with a full course load of eighteen units and a commitment to volleyball. Between her academics and extracurricular activities, she didn't have a lot of time for me. Most couples would have taken this change in stride, as natural distance in the relationship, as temporary sacrifice for future rewards. However, that's not where my head was at. I just kept thinking she was pulling away, fearing the worst.

I became self-consumed, obsessed with the fear of rejection to the point where I lacked the ability to recognize anybody else's needs. The fear was overwhelming me, and I started trying to coerce Tamba into spending more time with me. My emotions were out of control. I continued to unravel and come apart. I kept wondering what was happening to me. I no longer knew who I was. The fear of rejection was tormenting me endlessly. Finally, I couldn't stand it anymore. I then called Tamba and told her that our relationship was in jeopardy and insisted that she make more time for us. When she didn't respond the way I wanted, I threatened to break up with her. This drove her to tears, so I said that I would give it another chance. It was a purely selfish act. My perception and understanding were so distorted that I was seeing everything through a lens of fear and rejection. Everything became about mitigating my emotions and the fear that was tormenting me. I would have done anything to change the way I was feeling. I was unable to understand the most reasonable demands on her time. I was so consumed by fear that it was crippling my ability to think rationally or even be reasonable about the other demands on her time.

Naturally, given Tamba's academic and athletic commitments, she was unable to give me the attention I wanted. Nothing she could have said or done would have changed the insecurity I was experiencing. Something else in me had taken over. Fear was clearly in the driver's seat, and it seemed determined to drive me off a cliff into the rocks below. After a few weeks with no apparent changes in her time commitments, I called her up and broke it off. It was a desperate and coercive act of manipulation that came out of extreme immaturity, and I hurt her deeply. She broke down in tears in the middle of a volleyball tournament and drove back to San Diego that night to see her mother. Only later did I understand the impact of my actions, and it filled me with grief. I had committed a heinous sin against her that I would later learn could not be remedied.

Suddenly I was filled with grief and extreme remorse. I felt a terrible condemnation come over me. *How could I have done such a horrible thing to the woman I love? How could I break her heart for my own selfish ends?* Now I was in the grip of anxiety and feeling self-condemned. Drowning in my emotions, I was like a man floundering in waves of the sea, driven and tossed by the wind. I was adrift, floating in a sea of torment, trying to grab onto anything that might keep me afloat. I sought to make restitution immediately. I tried to call her so I could make things right, but her mother stood in the gap, her voice firm, a little icy, protective. She told me that Tamba didn't want to talk at the moment. There was nothing I could do. I had hit a wall, and it was insurmountable.

It hit me that it was really and truly over. I was sinking into deep despair. I was descending into an emotional abyss filled with my worst nightmares, and I had no idea how to pull myself out. I had deceived myself into thinking that if she really understood that our very relationship was at stake, that she would somehow come around, put everything else on the back burner, and make me her number one priority. Though I had feigned the threat of breaking up, this foolish stunt had proved fatal to the relationship. After her trust was shattered, we could never again have complete restoration as a couple. It was over, completely and permanently. This realization hit me like a wrecking ball. *Tamba was everything a man could want, and I alone sabotaged and destroyed the relationship.* My fear had become a self-fulfilling prophecy. Tamba was gone from my life, and how would I live with myself? Panic struck me like a red-hot iron in the chest. I literally felt like I was going to die, like my insides were being torn apart or being turned inside-out. With my heart beating out of my chest, I broke out in the sweats. I was physically, mentally, and emotionally on overload. My worst nightmare had come true. The woman of my dreams was no longer part of my life. I became sick, overwhelmed, and nauseated.

My relationship with Tamba had revealed what had been in me all along. I was an immature, sick, broken man filled with darkness and I didn't know it. It was a fate worse than death itself. I was left alone with myself, and I was a miserable person to be with. I started to despise who I was, or what I had let myself become, yet I felt powerless to change myself or my circumstances.

Desperate for relief from my pain, guilt and shame, I first tried to meet with the pastor of the church we had been attending. Pastor Sable was a well-dressed, distinguished man with silver hair and spectacles. The poor man was completely unprepared for my total breakdown in his office. I sat there sobbing and overwhelmed with sorrow. My heart was broken. He just stared at me silent, not knowing what to do. He listened patiently as I poured my heart out. After I was finished, he prayed for me. I was desperate for answers, for some counsel, and I got none. His prayer sounded trite, even glib to me. I regretted sharing such intimate emotions and overwhelming grief with him. I was overwrought, needing answers and getting none.

Tamba returned to school late that weekend. I left base the following Friday and drove to Orange County to try and meet her at the dormitory. When I finally arrived at the college, I went straight to her dorm room to talk to her. My heart was beating out of my chest as I stood in front of her door. I knocked. When she answered the door, she came out into the hallway to hear what I had to say. After apologizing, I told her that I had made a big mistake and wanted to start over. She simply said, "David, I could never trust you again." I tried to reconcile with her a number of times. Flowers went into the trash, and my other attempts to make restitution only started to be perceived as pathetic groveling.

I then called Tamba's mother, Cheryl. I tried to explain myself and apologize for perpetrating such a foolish stunt. *Surely, Tamba's mother could see my sincerity and mediate an understanding between us.* Cheryl said that she would see what she could do, but she also warned me. She said that her daughter's heart had been broken by her father long ago, and that after this recent breakup it would be unlikely Tamba would risk having her heart broken again. Cheryl, gracious as she was and sensing my desperation, invited me to come over if I needed to talk. After I returned from Orange County, I arranged to see her as soon as I could. I left the base the following Friday evening. When I arrived, Cheryl sat me down and listened patiently as I gave a repeat breakdown of my most sincere regrets. Cheryl was very frank with me. She told me that Tamba had said that she would never trust me again.

The statement was final, like something cast in stone. I had put something into motion that would be unchangeable.

I began to feel fatigue as my mind refused to turn off. I could not stop thinking and reasoning. This conversation left me bombarded with feelings of self-loathing. I kept trying to come up with some solution, any answer. Then I would go back to condemning myself. I could feel how tired my brain was, but my mind wouldn't shut off. I was descending into darkness, and there was no pulling out of it. My next stop would take me to the *shadowlands*.

CHAPTER 10

Night of the Dark Soul

CHERYL GRACIOUSLY ALLOWED ME TO stay the night before going back to the base. I was allowed to sleep downstairs in a guest room. That night I grieved, sobbing into my pillow. Something had broken inside me. I was overwrought with despair, and the darkness seemed to close in on me. I was in a deep, dark hole and felt totally and utterly alone. Feeling panicked, trying to sleep was useless. My heart was beating out of my chest. I began to break out in sweats, tossing and turning fitfully all night. It was as though I were being tormented by unseen assailants, even by the very darkness itself. I was staring into a black abyss. The torment continued all night as I kept hearing in my head: *It's entirely your fault! There's no hope for you! Your life will never be the same! It's the end for you! You will never have a relationship, not like this one! Ever! Your life is ruined forever! You might as well end it now! Throw it away! Life is not going to be worth living! You had it all, and you just threw it away! It's all your fault!* All night long I continued to battle and fight the thoughts in my head, and sleep fled from me.

I got up the next morning with my bed sheets soaked. I was exhausted, and I felt like I'd been hit by a truck. My body felt heavy with the weight of the world. It was difficult to even breathe. I used the bathroom to clean up before heading back to Pendleton. As I was preparing to shave, I looked in the mirror. When I saw my face, something caught my eye. I looked again, this time more closely. No, it wasn't my imagination. I leaned in closer. I stared at myself. I held my gaze. Something was different. Something wasn't right. I looked again, long and hard into my face. *No,* I thought, *it couldn't be.* But I knew it was true. The light was gone from my eyes. I knew then that something was seriously wrong.

I returned to Pendleton feeling haggard. The last couple of weeks before getting out of the Corps, I functioned mechanically, going through the motions to continue working at the base. I was already starting to disengage from my Marine brothers, realizing that I would probably never see them again. My heart was aching and my mind was elsewhere as I anticipated my discharge date. Life seemed vacuous and lacked meaning for me. It became more about just surviving and continuing to function.

I had determined months earlier that I was going to Bible College after the Marine Corps. Ironically, even in my current condition I was convinced that God had called me to the ministry. I knew that I was an emotional mess inside, but I desperately needed direction and structure after the Corps, and I knew that Bible College would give me that. This time I had no plan B. No contingency plan. Consequently, my course was set. I would be attending Pacific Christian College in Fullerton, the same college Tamba was attending. Considering my desperate emotional state, the thought of going into ministry was laughable at this point. *Am I kidding myself?* Maybe I was. I knew that I was still sinking, but I needed something to hang onto. I had nothing else left.

CHAPTER 11

Last Ditch Prayer

IT TOOK ME TWO WEEKS to process out of the military. I received my honorable discharge on November 14ᵀᴴ, 1987. I had already missed the fall semester and wouldn't be starting college until the spring of '88. That would give me several weeks before the school semester started. After my discharge I moved back into my mother's house. I was an emotional wreck and I knew it. My heart was broken. I was still very much in despair, living with this black cloud over me. Anxiety still plagued me, and I lived with a constant sense of impending doom, like the other shoe was about to drop at any moment. I was merely surviving. I was existing, and God seemed a million miles away.

My emotional state kept worsening, and I knew that I was in a dangerous place emotionally. My former passivity had transformed into seething, controlled rage underneath my hurting exterior. I hated myself for what I had allowed myself to become. I was lost and in severe pain. There seemed to be no answers and no options. Idleness was my worst enemy at this time. It was during this interim period between my military discharge and my pending start date for college that I was feeling extremely restless. I continued going to my local church and attended some of the services. I remember the pastor teaching about the Spirit leading Jesus into the wilderness to fast for forty days and forty nights. After the service I talked to a number of people I hadn't seen for a while, catching up on their news and trying to avoid the question, "How are you doing?"

Afterward, I thought more about the pastor's message. Then the thought came to me, *fasting!* I thought, *Jesus fasted! Didn't a lot of people in the Bible fast when they needed answers? Seems I remember stories of wars being won and prayers being answered when people fasted. That's it! I will begin a three-day fast –water only! I'll begin fasting and praying for some answers from God!* I had never fasted in my life. The thought had never even occurred to me until then. I considered this a big deal. I had heard of men and women in the Bible fasting when they were in a crisis, and God always answered them. People always seemed to get some form of breakthrough when they fasted and prayed. Being all out of options, I decided that I would fast for three days and three nights to get an answer. I thought, *Who knows, maybe God will intervene on my behalf and speak to Tamba sovereignly.* Since there was no wilderness in the middle of the metropolitan area of Orange County, I decided that I would spend three days and three nights in my Mustang at a nearby park. I explained to my mom what I was doing and why. Then I packed my pillow and some blankets and left.

> *"The Lord is near the broken hearted, and He saves those who are crushed in spirit."* Psalm 34:18 NAS

Dotted with an assortment of deciduous trees, Mile Square Park was one complete square mile of green grass, ponds, and soft hills. On one side of the park was an inlet for parking that had a couple of tennis courts and two cinder block restrooms with drinking fountains - all I would need for my three day appeal to God. I pulled into the lot, found a spot underneath a shade tree, and parked my car. My face contorted, and I broke down and cried against the steering wheel. The pain was deep and excruciating. Now that there was no distraction, the pain and despair seemed all consuming. My crying soon became sobbing, and then my sobbing became wailing. I gathered up a towel and held it over my mouth to muffle the sound. The pain was deep and raw. My nose began to run. The flood gates were open and there was no stopping it.

As twilight came, I was once again tormented by my self-condemnation. *How did I end up here, so desperate and miserable and sleeping in my car? Honestly, I never saw it coming. But I should have. After all, I'm the one who sabotaged my career in law enforcement. I'm the one who sabotaged a relationship with the girl of my dreams. Come to think of it, I've failed at everything I've ever tried. I'm sick, very sick. There is really nothing left for me here, and this pain in my soul is unbearable. I can't take this anymore...I could end it though...I could end it all right now. Why not?*

Thoughts of a future without the woman I loved left me void, feeling lonely and destitute. Thoughts of my failure projected visions of being homeless and walking the streets. I cried on and off for hours. That night went on forever. I was still being torn up inside. As the sun went down and darkness closed in, the pain became even more excruciating. I cried out to God, begging Him to take away the pain, but it would not abate. I began to seriously contemplate suicide, anything to escape the depth of agony and the overwhelming sense of loss I was experiencing at that moment. I thought of how I might do it. *How would I kill myself?* My mind drifted as I thought about the people who care about me...*Who really cared about me? Seems like everyone is caught up with their own problems. Nobody could help me anyway. How would I do it? How would I take my life?* My mind drifted back. I thought about what it was like growing up.

Then out of nowhere, a Bible verse popped into my mind. *"If any man destroys the temple of God, God will destroy him, for the temple of God is holy, and that is what you are."* I Corinthians 3:17

Time suddenly stopped...I knew right at that moment God had spoken directly to me. This kept me from seriously taking any suicidal action. I was already destroyed. I didn't need to take my life only to have God destroy it again. I pursued the thought no further, and that was the end of the matter. I could only remain in the crucible of my pain. Again I tried to breathe and only did so with great effort. Everything took effort. The grief I felt was as if someone very close to me had died. In some respect that would have been easier to deal with. At least I would not have been at fault, to bear the full weight of the blame and guilt. All I could do was to breathe and survive the next moment alone in my car. I cried out to God for mercy. "Please God! It hurts! It hurts! It hurts…" My voice trailed off as I weakened in despair. Each time I would begin praying only to be interrupted by a crescendo of tears and sobbing. I would get a moment of reprieve only to have the weight of my pain and loss crash in on me again. This distress continued throughout the first day and night. I begged God for mercy, to bring Tamba back into my life and take away the pain. "Please bring her back, God! Please bring her back. Take away the pain, God." On and on I cried into the night.

My grieving was suddenly interrupted. One of the park maintenance workers told me that the park closed at ten o'clock; this meant that I would need to find a place to sleep for the night. I quickly decided to find a church parking lot to bed down for the evening. I cruised around Fountain Valley looking for a church with a parking lot that would accommodate me. I soon found what looked like an old-style church with a pitched roof. I pulled in around the back of it. The lot was dark, expansive, and quiet. Perfect for catching a few winks. I drove to the far corner of the lot and parked in the shadows, avoiding what little exterior lighting there was. I was very tired. I hadn't been sleeping well to begin with, and grieving was exhausting me. Moreover, I hadn't eaten anything all day. My stomach kept turning and growling in protest. I didn't drink any water because I didn't want to have to use a restroom. I thought I would just try to get some sleep, so I cranked my seat all the way back and closed my eyes and fell fast asleep.

One hour later, I awakened with a start by tapping on my windshield and two blinding flashlights in my eyes. Squinting, I held one hand up shielding my eyes from the glare. The two officers ordered me out of the car. They asked me who I was and what I was doing there. Then they asked me to produce my license and registration. I complied. Their car continued to idle while their spotlights lit up my car like a showcase. One officer shined his flashlight down on my license while the other kept his light on me. I must have looked like a homeless person standing in the cold night air in my socks. My five o'clock shadow now had a full day and a half of growth, and I was feeling scruffy.

"Someone called us," the officer said, "We got a complaint from a church member." Then he said, "You don't have any business here, so you need to leave."

"Just trying to find a place to sleep," I said.

"Well you can't stay here; you need to go," he said abruptly.

"Well, where do I go?" I asked.

With finality the officer retorted, "Anywhere outside Fountain Valley." After returning my wallet and registration, the officers stood by while I got back into my car and drove off the lot.

I was determined to complete this fast without distraction, so I decided on a place that would be less conspicuous. I settled for a big box store parking lot. It was a lot busier, but I figured among all the other cars I would be left alone. My sleep was broken throughout the evening, interrupted by sounds of the night, the intermittent and muted sounds of people talking, car doors slamming, and young teens whooping it up as they passed by. That first night my sleep was broken, fitful, and I got very little rest.

I awoke the next morning with a pounding headache from caffeine deprivation. I collected myself at daybreak and headed back to the park. I found the same spot under the shade tree.

After parking, I ambled over to the cinder block restrooms, but they were still locked. I went back to the car and waited. My heart was heavy, and my feet felt like lead. I started to ask God why I had to lose Tamba. Once again, crying out, I asked Him to intervene, to bring her back into my life. Then, for the second time since my fast started, God spoke to me. *David, you made this relationship into an idol. There will be no false gods before Me. The pain you are experiencing is the result of that sin. The relationship became a stumbling block for you. For that reason, I cannot give her to you.* I sat there stunned. God had spoken, and I knew His voice right away! It was all true, and the truth was sobering. The pain in my soul reverberated within me. I continued to fast, pray, and grieve throughout my second day, hoping that God would change His mind, though deep within I knew I already had my answer. I couldn't admit that there was no chance left.

I persevered in fasting and prayer, but as I did so, my prayer began to take on another focus. I began to see clearly the depth of my brokenness and the need for change in my life. My old façade had been shattered into a million pieces. I felt like Humpty Dumpty, and I knew that all the king's horses and all the king's men could not put me back together again. It would take the King Himself to do it. For the first time in my life I was realizing that I was not only unfit for a relationship in any romantic context, but I was emotionally crippled. Unless God did something extraordinary in my life, I would be unable to have a relationship...ever! Something deep inside me would need to change, and I was at a total loss as to how to change it.

Later, my headache began to wane and level off. Something was broken deep inside me, and I knew that I couldn't fix it. I continued to pray that God would bring Tamba back into my life, only now I was also asking Him to fix my brokenness, to take away the pain in my life. I recognized that I was helpless to do anything to change myself. I would need a new heart. I would need a new soul. In other words, I would need a miracle. I realized that I was a walking black hole emotionally. I understood that without God's intervention I would remain hopelessly broken beyond remedy. I knew my brokenness would destroy any potential success in my life. I also knew that my neediness would ultimately sabotage and destroy any future prospect for relationship, and that my very future hung in the balance. This revelation now gave my prayer and fasting a dual purpose. Though I knew in the core of my being what God's decision was regarding Tamba, my heart still could not let go. I was in bondage to my desire, chained to what once was. I continued to grieve and call out to God throughout the second night.

At dawn the next morning, I left the store parking lot and drove back to the park. It was my third day without food. I noticed a white hatchback in my usual parking space, so I opted for a spot under a different tree. It was early, so there was plenty of parking. After washing up in the restroom I remained in my car throughout the day. The hunger pangs were more intense now. My only source of entertainment was watching an assortment of passersby: a man in his thirties jogged by in a blue jogging suit, a couple walking their dog, two women speed-walking...later, a bicyclist sped by. I chose not to listen to any radio for the full three days. I wanted to focus my full attention on God, and I didn't want anything distracting me from hearing His voice. I wanted answers, and I was willing to give up anything to get them. I continued to fast, pray and call out to God. I waited...waited for some answer. God was now silent. He had already spoken, and I knew His words were final. I began to consider what I might do to facilitate my own recovery. For the next few weeks at least, I would be surviving rather than living, struggling to function in the midst of my pain and loss. I was feeling vulnerable, tender, exposed. Throughout the third day, I continued to grieve, and though I was still feeling broken and hungry, I had a distinct sense that God had heard my plea.

As evening finally came to a close on the third day, I began to feel discouraged again. I would be going home tomorrow, getting ready for my first college semester. My fast would be over, and I still had not gotten the answer I had hoped for. I began to reflect on the answers I did receive over the last three days. Based on what God had told me, I knew that I was in no way allowed to take my own life. Even the very thought was no longer a consideration. He also told me that a relationship with Tamba was off the table. My last request for healing still remained unanswered; however, I knew that God's answer would not provide a quick fix.

In the midst of my pain, I was experiencing something different, something I couldn't put my finger on at the moment. As my fast neared its end, the stubble on my face was beginning to itch, and I was beginning to see visions of double cheese burgers and pizza slices floating in the air around me. As I pulled into the shopping center's parking lot, I looked for a place on the outskirts of the majority of the cars that were already parked. Once I parked the Mustang, I wrenched my seat all the way back, threw a blanket over myself, and went to sleep.

PART II

A Journey of Deliverance

CHAPTER 12

Accepted!

SOMETHING HAD CHANGED, AND I could feel it. Something was different. The difference was subtle at first. I arrived home early the next morning with an awareness that I possessed something that I didn't have three days ago. It was hope. There was an assurance that came from the conviction that God was with me, and I was not alone. I broke my fast with a very large breakfast consisting of scrambled eggs, bacon, toast, and a cup of coffee. I showered, shaved, and cleaned up. I spent the next two weeks getting ready for the spring semester of college. The very word *college* intimidated me. I grew up hating school. For the most part, it had been an all-around negative experience. School had always been a hostile environment. Schoolwork was a struggle, so much so, I barely graduated. Consequently, I never had any intention of returning. Graduation felt like the end of a long prison term. *Why would I ever want to go back to school?* I reasoned that this would be a Christian school and a different experience altogether.

Something had changed me in the last four years. I had developed a hunger, a thirst for knowledge. I had a desire for answers, a desire to learn, and I was filled with questions. I felt a call and a desire to serve God in ministry. This focus gave me a new-found purpose, and God used it to change my heart toward academics and learning. I actually wanted to go back to school; it had to be God!

My dad always told me: "David you can do anything in this life that you want to do if you only have the interest." This truth was clear in my boyhood as I would fixate on every new hobby, interest, and project. My tendency toward obsession became evident with every new interest I took up from dinosaurs, rocks, lizards, model airplanes, rockets, ants, rats, and snakes. When I was into something, it was all consuming. I would get so excited about my new interest that it would be all I could talk about to the consternation of my family. Every new project seemed to dominate my interest, time, and attention. I had no trouble learning about anything that fascinated me.

Conversely, when I lacked interest in a school subject I seemed unable to retain any information about it at all. Dad said that I had selective memory. Mom said I had selective hearing. Truth be told, it was subjects like Home Economics and Latin American history that seemed like irrelevant and useless information in contrast to my struggle to survive life and the decimation of my family. This was especially true when it came to mathematics. I was a senior in high school when I finally learned my timetables. My focus was clearly elsewhere. If I had a gene missing, it had to be the quantitative thought gene. Dad would spend late nights drilling me for a test. Granted, his teaching techniques probably left a lot to be desired, but at least he cared enough to try! This had to be exasperating for him, spending late nights drilling me after a long day of work only to have me flunk my exam the next day. I seemed unable to remember the second step in any formula, and this kept me from ever moving beyond pre-algebra.

Not having developed my academic skills, I knew that college would be a challenge for me. I had already figured that by the time I'd be starting my first semester, I would be twenty-five years old, well above the median age of most of the student body. I was excited about college, but quite frankly intimidated by it given my poor academic history. However, I was fairly confident that I would enjoy the atmosphere of a Christian college. I was also reasonably sure that a Christian college would not be a hangout for the rowdy types that I had contended with in high school.

Nevertheless, the prospect of graduating with a bachelor's degree in ministry seemed daunting. I knew that what lay ahead could soon overwhelm me without good planning. I needed a good strategy. Here was my strength. I had always been analytical. So I would do the only thing that I knew how to do. I would plan, organize and strategize my success in advance.

When I thought of my goal and how overwhelming it seemed, I simply stopped thinking about it. I knew that I could get easily overwhelmed, so I pushed the thought out of my mind. I then broke my goal down into its smallest pieces, its tiniest parts. I decided that I would concern myself with *only* the next step, whatever that might be. Consequently, I would forget about everything else until it became absolutely necessary. My first task was to gather information about my college of choice. I soon discovered that there was a fringe benefit to focusing on my plan for college. It helped me to redirect my thoughts about Tamba. This enabled me to function. It helped me cope with the ever present pain by giving me a distraction. This allowed me to channel my energy into more constructive endeavors.

Though I lacked the GPA to attend Pacific Christian College, and likely lacked the academic skills to succeed, I would continue to break down my goal into its smallest parts. Someone once told me: "If you want to eat an elephant, you've got to eat it one bite at a time." This proverb had always stuck with me. Any task, however daunting, could be made manageable by simply breaking it down into much smaller increments. My first step would be to make a phone call to the college. My second step would be to gather as much information as I could get my hands on. That first phone call gave me the next few steps I would need to begin attending this school.

The first time I stepped onto the campus of Pacific Christian College in Fullerton, California, I sensed excitement in the air. I took some time to survey the campus. The central part of the campus consisted of the executive and faculty offices as well as the library. The architecture looked like some kind of futuristic starship with three spires jutting out from the front of the building. A broad stairway led up to the library on the second floor. From this central location, wide concrete walkways spanned out in all directions. The longest and broadest of these walkways was lined with lampposts and led straight to the dormitories. This walkway also bordered the parking lot. Green grass areas were intermittent between the walkways. Classrooms surrounded the main building, all two stories high. The dormitories were two buildings separated by an upstairs cafeteria and a large swimming pool. On one side were the men's dorms and on the other, the women's. Both dormitories had large common areas, each with its own fireplace centered in the lobby. The atmosphere on campus, all in all, seemed bright and cheery. I went to the office and met the young receptionist I had talked to on the phone. I then walked over to the financial aid office, where the staff could not have been more helpful. They assisted me in applying for every possible loan, grant, and scholarship that I was eligible for. I couldn't help but notice the kind service and the favor I was given. When my loan was approved, I was quickly notified.

A week later I was called in for an academic review with the college principal. This made me a little nervous since none of my experiences in principal's offices had ever ended well for me. When I arrived for my appointment, Principal Montgomery invited me into his office. I kept trying to read the air, bracing myself for the worst. I knew there was a good chance that my application would be rejected because of my poor academic history. I sat down opposite a large expansive desk. There was no wall behind him, only a large floor-to-ceiling window overlooking the whole campus. Shelves filled with books lined both sides of his office. I immediately felt way out of my league.

Principal Montgomery stood as we shook hands, "Please have a seat Mr. Jacques." "David. You can call me David," I said. We both sat down. Then he said, "Tell me a little bit about yourself, David."

"Well, I've been a Christian for five years. After coming to Christ, I felt a call to share the message of Christ in the military with the Marines. So I enlisted. I've been overseas twice. Over the last four years, I've only had a stronger conviction that I am called to serve God in ministry. After considerable thought and prayer, I decided to go to a Bible college. Pacific Christian College is associated with the denomination that led me to Christ, and it's also close to Garden Grove, where I grew up. So I feel prompted to attend here."

He began shuffling some paperwork on his desk. Then leaned back in his chair holding up what looked like a transcript in front of him.

"David, I have to be honest with you. It's unusual for us to accept students with the kind of grade point average you have in your high school records. That's why I wanted to meet you first and talk with you personally. This institution has very high scholastic standards and is extremely rigorous in its academic coursework. It's not my desire to set you, or anybody else, up for failure. My concern is that you might find our coursework more challenging than what you are currently equipped to handle... have you considered maybe starting at a community college first and then later transferring?"

I leaned forward in my chair for emphasis. "Mr. Montgomery, I haven't been in high school for six years. I think I have matured considerably since then. I have a very specific goal, and I intend to take my education very seriously. Just give me a chance to prove myself."

Mr. Montgomery just sat there, tapping on his desk with the back of his pen, looking at me. I could see that he was in the process of making a decision. Then, after a brief moment of reflection, he said, "I'll tell you what...we will accept your application on the condition of your performance. You will be given six months of academic probation, at which time we will review your grades to determine whether you will be allowed to continue."

He signaled that our meeting was over by standing. I followed suit and stood with him. He smiled as he extended his hand, "Welcome aboard. Good luck to you." Leaving his office I said, "Thank you, sir!"

I ran out of his office, past the library and down the stairs more excited than ever. I was accepted, and I knew God was with me! I was actually excited! This small victory was a welcome reprieve from my current challenges. However, little did I know that God was about to take me through a crucible of testing.

CHAPTER 13

The Crucible

Cru-ci-ble: 1. a container in which metals are purified using very high temperatures. 2. A place or occasion of severe test or trial. 3. A situation in which different variables interact to catalyze something new.

GOING FROM THE BARBARITY OF the Marine Corps to attend a Christian College was quite a culture shock. My first year of college would prove to be more challenging than anything I had experienced in the Corps, testing me beyond anything I'd ever experienced in my life, and that's saying something! While the academics were rigorous, the spiritual test was far greater. It only occurred to me as I was settling into my dorm that I really hadn't thought through the challenges of attending the same college as Tamba. It then dawned on me just how difficult this was going to be!

The rushed pace that began spring semester kept my mind busy and temporarily muted my emotional pain. Even in the midst of all the hustle and bustle of students getting settled into their dormitories, fear and anxiety still plagued me. The absence of light in my eyes served as a reminder that something was still very broken inside me. Being at a loss as to what to do about it, I just busied myself with the myriad of things that needed to get done before the first classes started. In addition to moving into the dorm, I started a job working for campus security. My responsibilities were to make sure that all the classrooms were locked and secure at the end of classes each day. The work helped pay for my room and board.

I was still getting used to my new surroundings when I turned a corner by the campus bookstore, and there she was. My heart jolted as fear stabbed me like a sharp knife. I caught my breath and said, "Hi." She gave a silent, obligatory wave as she continued by with some friends. Every time I saw her I experienced all the rejection and abandonment all over again. Somehow, all memories of rejection I had ever experienced in my life were transferring to this relationship. Something about this whole breakup had traumatized me, like some form of post-traumatic stress, releasing all the pain in my past. I recognized that my reaction was irrational. Something was very wrong with me, and I knew it. Every encounter was another reminder of my failure as a man.

The first day of classes started and my first class was World Civilization. The book for the class was a thick, heavy hardcover with a dense commentary, and accounted for most of the weight in my backpack. When I entered the classroom I sat toward the front to avoid distractions. This was uncharacteristic of me because in high school I had always sat in the back. However, I now knew that I would have to do things differently than I had in the past. Other students filed in, filling in the seats around me. Just as class was scheduled to start, in walked in Mr. Montgomery, the schools' principal. I was surprised to learn that he would be teaching the class and also functioned as one of the professors. Principal Montgomery was tall, with a balding head of hair, and a salt and pepper mustache. He wore thick, black-rimmed glasses that seemed out-of-date and had a high forehead, no doubt to house that large computer brain he possessed.

I was immediately concerned and unsettled. He began his lecture by reviewing the course syllabus. He explained in rapid speech the course requirements and how it would involve three separate modules, each ending with an exam, and each worth 33 percent of our overall grade. As Mr. Montgomery continued his monologue, it felt like the oxygen had been sucked out of the room. I began to feel overwhelmed. The more he talked, the more I began to panic. I started noticing that many of the other students were taking notes on laptop computers. I didn't even own a computer – never had! I scribbled notes like a kid with a crayon. Even writing as fast as I could, I couldn't keep up. My heart began to race, and I began to perspire as all I could hear was the droning of Mr. Montgomery's voice with the non-stop clicking of computer keys in the background. I was feeling anxious and overwhelmed. *I need to get out of here! I'm not ready for this!*

It was total panic! When class was over, I made a beeline for the door. I went straight to the administration office to drop the class like a kid playing with a handful of red ants. I clearly wasn't ready for it. I stood by the elevator. When it opened, there stood Mrs. Ferrell, one of the other professors I recognized. Both she and her husband, Mr. Ferrell, were new additions to the faculty, and the college was delighted to have them on staff. She was a vivacious, middle-aged, blond lady with short curly hair. As the elevator door closed, she could see the panic on my face.

"Oh dear, something wrong?"

The elevator continued to bump and glide down to the ground floor. I proceeded to unload on her. "I just got out of Mr. Montgomery's World Civ class. It's my first college semester. I'm on academic probation. He talks really fast. I'm not ready to take a course like this. I can't afford to fail any classes, so I'm going downstairs to drop this class!"

Without skipping a beat Mrs. Ferrell chirped, "Then take my class instead."

"What class would that be?" I asked.

"I'm teaching Poetic Analysis!" she bounced, clapping her hands together. "You'll pass my class, no problem!"

My panic began to subside, the crisis suddenly over. I thanked her profusely, and quickly returned to admissions where I switched classes. I knew that I would eventually have to take Mr. Montgomery's class since it was a course requirement, but I also knew that first I would need time to acclimate to academic life by taking the easier classes first. Consequently, I would seek to buy time (literally, at $120 a unit). Once I had gained my academic "legs," I would then start taking the more difficult courses. That was the plan anyway.

The following day I got to Mrs. Ferrell's Poetic Analysis class early. I sat up front, as was becoming my custom. I was turned facing the door, watching the other students file in, and there was Tamba. Tamba had the same class! My heart raced as I began to think of all the potential ways I could look stupid in front of her. *Now she would see first-hand how slow and inept I really am. Great!* I tried to calm myself. She had taken a seat to the rear and left of me. Tamba was confident and completely in her element. In contrast, I felt like a ship in the desert. My academic skills were rusty at best. No problem. I would merely listen, observe, and take notes. I would remain silent to avoid even saying anything that might sound stupid.

That, unfortunately, was not going to work, because as it turned out, Mrs. Ferrell was big on class participation, and she would call on students frequently. Fortunately, she was also a wise woman. I think someone had made her privy to my falling out with Tamba, or perhaps she had seen my old transcripts or knew about my probationary status. Whatever it was, she seemed to intuitively know how vulnerable I was feeling. I sensed that she was careful about the questions she asked me in class.

Several weeks had passed when I saw Tamba walking hand-in-hand with some other guy. To say that I was shocked, hurt, and dismayed would not come close to describing the depth of pain that shot through me at that moment. That was it! It was more than I could take. I was sick to my stomach. I had to get away, anything to escape this nagging pain in my soul. I began taking immediate action to transfer to another college. My goal was to get a bachelor's degree in ministry, so I sought another Christian college. I first tried to transfer to Biola University but discovered their extremely high tuition fees. I realized that this was no longer an option, so I turned my attention to Calvary Chapel Bible College at Twin Peaks. This too proved to be a dead end for me because the college would not accept government-assisted loans or grants; so although the tuition fees were more affordable, I still could not afford to attend. Consequently, I was stuck in this crucible of torment.

Worse than that, the guy she was with was nothing like me. I was a tall, clean shaven, A-J squared away, former Marine. This guy was a shorter man, slight of build, with a scraggly beard, and a weak chin. Being my total opposite, I figured that he must be a brain like she was, and that is what they shared in common. However, none of that really mattered now because I was stuck here, trapped in my circumstance. I would remain imprisoned in this fiery furnace of emotional torment for the next four years. Hoorah!

I knew that as a Christian I was supposed to love everybody. I also knew that this guy Tamba was dating was likely my brother in the faith. Nevertheless, I didn't like him, and the feelings were mutual. I figured that Tamba had surely filled him in on who I was and our history together. Occasionally, sneers would be exchanged as we both reverted to acting like adolescents. That whole semester my emotions vacillated between despair and rage, feeling repentant one moment and then wanting to retaliate in my burning anger the next. I imagined slashing all four of Tamba's tires with my Ka-bar and setting her car on fire but never acted on the impulse. I knew that I was broken beyond repair, and by the end of my first semester I was bitter and cynical. I began to bury myself in academics for escape. God, however, had other plans.

CHAPTER 14

Divine Appointment

I'VE ALWAYS BELIEVED THAT GOD is in total control of *everything*, and that He is like a cosmic master chess player, actively moving and manipulating circumstances on the chess board of life to bring about His will and purposes for our good. Doubt would only arise when I would make the mistake of presuming that my will and purposes were the same as His.

In spite of the emotional challenges, I was able to channel my nervous energy into my academic pursuits. To my surprise, the result was a near 3.0 GPA! In addition to my full-time commitment as a Bible college student, I had been attending Bible studies four to five nights a week at Calvary Chapel in Costa Mesa. At the time, it was an all-star lineup of great Bible teachers: Greg Laurie, Oden Fong, Pastor Chuck Smith, and Chuck Missler. Moreover, there were often Saturday night concerts with various guest speakers, and I attended as often as I could.

I reasoned that if I could saturate myself with enough Bible verses, it would somehow *fix* me. I was taught that if you had any personal problems or character defects, all you needed was more of God's Word in you. I was told that the Scriptures would renew and fix everything, and that the more Bible you knew, the more spiritually mature you were. At least that was my understanding. It was for this reason that I sought to get as much Bible inside my brain as I could squeeze in there. Between full-time Bible College and my nightly Bible studies throughout the week, I had the Bible coming out of my ears. Unfortunately, all this Bible study did not bring about the desired result. I still was very broken inside.

"...Knowledge makes arrogant, but love edifies"
1 Corinthians 8:1 NAS

My Bible knowledge had become another fortress for me to hide behind, and I began to take pride and get my value in how well I knew the Bible. My heart eventually became hard and cynical, and I began to become puffed up. I even began arguing with the professors in class, trying to win them toward my theological perspective. I would try to correct them and show them where they were wrong. Imagine the arrogance! I became critical and rough with my words. This, of course, didn't win over anybody but only served to make me more odious in the eyes of the faculty and my fellow students. Truth can be brutal when it's not tempered with love and compassion. Needless to say, I didn't become very popular with the faculty. In spite of my immaturity and rough edges, people were still patient with me. I'm sure that they could see what I couldn't. They understood that I was someone who required extra grace.

It was the beginning of my second year of college when I met him. I was walking across the campus toward the men's dorms when I looked up and saw a man walking away at a distance in the opposite direction. He was about my height. He had blue eyes, shoulder-length brown hair and a beard. At first I thought he looked like Jesus. When he looked up, our eyes met. As though there was some divine purpose for it, the man suddenly changed direction and came toward me. As he drew closer, he began to look more like Keith Green than Jesus.

When he got to where I was standing, he stuck out his hand and said, "Hi! I'm Steve Hampton."

As we shook hands I said, "David Jacques, nice to meet you."

We talked for a while, and I learned that Steve had attended the college in the mid-seventies during the height of the "Jesus People" movement. At that time Steve and others thought Jesus would be returning at any moment to claim His church, so he dropped out of college his third year and moved to Hawaii to start a church. Steve said that he was with the Vineyard. That name didn't mean anything to me at that moment, but I found out that Steve had pastored a church for a number of years in Hawaii. It was only years later that he came back to the mainland to finish his last year of college and complete his degree.

Steve was in his forties when I met him. Steve was likeable and charismatic, and I discovered that he was a gifted musician and guitarist. It didn't take long before I realized that there was something very different about Steve. Unusual "things" would happen when Steve was around, things that I soon began to realize were supernatural. He turned out to be an extraordinary man, and God would use him to change the course of my life and the lives of others.

When I met Steve, he told me that he and a number of other students were meeting in his dorm for worship in the evenings and invited me to join them. Something told me that I needed to go. When I went looking for Steve's dorm room, I found it at the end of the hallway. This was significant because the dorm rooms at the ends of the buildings were much larger than the rest. This made them perfect for entertaining small groups. Steve would begin worship around 4:00 pm. People joined the group as their schedules permitted. Worship continued until the curfew, when the dorms would be closed to the opposite sex for the night.

What I didn't realize then was that Steve was selecting people for these gatherings based on divine guidance, and that our meeting was not by happenstance. God certainly knew my desperate condition. Meeting Steve Hampton was a divine appointment.

CHAPTER 15

The Gathering

I DIDN'T YET KNOW THIS, but God was about to move in some dramatic ways. When I first arrived at Steve's dorm there was a small gathering of students present. As they introduced themselves, I didn't know that I was meeting the people God would use to shape my life over the next four years. These people would become family to me throughout my time in college.

Steve was an anointed worshipper, and as we continued worshipping together on a regular basis I started to notice *things* happening whenever Steve would play his guitar. For instance, different individuals from time to time would break down crying. The first time it happened, I thought the tears were coming from someone who was just having a bad day. However, as different individuals at different times and in different places would break down in tears, I started noticing that the common denominator was Steve worshipping with his guitar or praying. I discerned that there was more going on than someone merely having a bad day or displaying frivolous emotionalism. There was an anointing on this man. I began to perceive that something supernatural was going on. Sometimes Steve would spontaneously give "words" to people with the result that they would feel a deep emotional impact. One thing was obvious: the Spirit of God was on Steve.

I wouldn't know until later that God was speaking to Steve and telling him specifically who he was to gather together and disciple. God was moving powerfully in our midst, and we didn't immediately realize it. Most of the time as we worshiped together, we were just experiencing a sweet, warm, atmosphere of love and acceptance. I began noticing that a heavy peace would settle in the air at the end of these prolonged periods of worship. Steve also seemed to know what God was saying and would speak over us now and then.

We continued gathering to worship, and more people began to join us. Over time, a small core of us became intimate friends, even like family. So much so, that I would never forget them.

One of the first of these students I met was Tim Gray. A big Texan, standing at six feet five inches tall, Tim was displaced from his home state after joining the Coast Guard. Later he traveled with the military to California. When he became a believer, he was convinced that the most serious response to his faith would be to attend a Christian Bible college. He was a gentle giant, easy-going and very wise, and would always ask profound questions that forced you to think a little deeper about a given subject. Tim eventually became a leader and a mentor in our group.

Lisa Doty was a third generation missionary kid who grew up in the Philippines. Being an international student, she studied linguistics and had an openness to new things as well as an appreciation for other cultures. Even with her cultured background, Lisa always appeared to me as a wholesome, all-American girl from the Midwest. She was very kind and diligently studious.

Then there was Todd Foerch, my roommate. Todd was tall, red-haired and freckled. He was an ambulance driver who decided to go to Bible College to answer a call to ministry. Todd had a quick wit and was quite the practical joker. Todd had a comedic persona and could always be counted on to lighten the mood when conversation became too heavy. Todd also had a radical faith in God and literally believed that all things were possible.

Karen Schooner was a thin, nineteen year old sophomore with long, red hair. A little shy, she often wore a smile on her kind face and was always a ray of sunshine and encouragement when you needed it. Gentle and quiet, Karen was a deep soul who seemed to exude the love and peace of God.

Steve Burger was a psychology major. He came to college as an older student and, like Steve Hampton, was also in his forties. Steve also had a background in ministry. Life experience had given Steve a treasure trove of wisdom that we all drew from as he spoke into our lives as an older brother and mentor.

Derek Morita was a native islander from Hawaii. Derek was a surfer and former drama student in high school. He was intelligent, analytical, and passionate. I always enjoyed his impersonations of various movie and TV personalities. The best was Captain Kirk of the Starship Enterprise. He seemed to have his voice inflections and mannerisms down pat.

Arthur Andrews came to Bible College to answer a call to ministry. Arthur was of Polish descent. He came to the United States when he was very young when his parents emigrated from Denmark. His sharp mind eventually put him in the category of gifted students. When he received a scholarship, he enrolled in Pacific Christian College and would eventually become a faithful and trusted friend to me and others.

Then there was J-Michael Wuestemann, another student I met on campus some time later. J-Michael was a radical Christian. Time and time again, he would demonstrate a level of faith that would constantly challenge me and stretch the limits of my faith. He had a strong prophetic gift, and demonstrated boldness for God. Never shy to approach others, I would see him on numerous occasions give astounding words of prophecy as God directed him.

These people would become the instruments God would use to shape my life and future in the most profound ways. He would use them to channel His love and healing into my life. As the weeks passed, our relationships grew and we developed deep bonds that seemed extraordinary to me. We became family to each other, family in the truest sense of the term. A love grew between us as friends, and that love allowed each of us to be truly honest with each other.

There was a purity and honesty in these relationships that came out of a heart of love. It was the love evident in the hearts of this group that would afford us the opportunity to speak directly into each other's lives without the need to push away, insulate ourselves, or react defensively. That made the quality of these relationships so rare.

God's truth, spoken prophetically in love through others, brought to each of us God's healing touch throughout college. This healing began to be evident as we continued worshipping together. God started gently softening our hearts, exposing our inconsistencies and the things in our character that were not pleasing to Him. God was getting us ready. However, we had no idea what was about to happen. God was preparing us to receive something that would change our lives forever.

CHAPTER 16

The Anointing

IT WAS THE MOST UNUSUAL night. We were all gathered together in Steve's dorm room. We had been worshipping for some time when the curfew hour arrived requiring girls to leave the room. We all wanted to continue worshipping, so Steve asked me to open up one of the classrooms to continue our time together. Since I was part of the security staff and had been entrusted with the keys, I opened one of the classrooms at the far end of campus to minimize any disturbance to other students.

The classroom on the second floor was dark and empty. We decided to leave the lights off not just for atmosphere, but also for discretion. We didn't want to be interrupted. The classroom was on the street side of the college, so we had plenty of light coming in through the window from the streetlamps. We all sat in front of this very large classroom in a semi-circle on the carpet with our legs crossed. There was a short, six inch, carpeted platform in front that Steve sat on as he played his guitar. We were all worshipping softly, giving praise to God and lifting up our voices. After we had been singing together for some time, Steve softly ended the last song. Then Steve said something that would forever change our lives. He put his guitar down and said,

"God spoke to me, and He told me that He would like you all to know Him in a very special way. So I want you all to hold out your hands like you're about to receive something."

We all extended our hands, resting them on our knees, palms up. As we sat there with our eyes closed, Steve spoke the words, "Holy Spirit, come!"

As we sat there waiting in silence, my torso suddenly began to involuntarily move and bob back and forth. *What!* I immediately opened my eyes to see who was touching me. I glanced to both sides of me. I was sitting between two girls and neither of them was touching me. I was slightly freaked out,

"Steve, I'm moving! What's going on?"

Steve held up his hand, "Relax, that's the Holy Spirit. The Holy Spirit comes in waves."

At that moment all I could think was: *Where in Scripture does it say that the Holy Spirit comes in waves?* Then I remembered the Bible verse where Jesus said that out of our innermost being will flow rivers of living water, and that the Holy Spirit is often compared to water in the Scriptures.

The others were feeling something as well, and the room was suddenly electric with excitement! Steve acted quickly saying, "Everybody, hold out your hands." Then he quickly went around the room praying for each of us to receive the gift of healing. He did this while resting his hands over our open palms. Steve encouraged us to start praying for people to get healed. Steve explained that when Jesus healed, He would lay His hands on people and that we should do the same.

In the aftermath of that meeting, I was reeling and blown away! *What had just happened? Was I just literally touched by God Himself? Did the living God of the universe just come down and invade the room and physically move me?* My mind continued reeling, trying to grasp what had just happened. I didn't yet fully comprehend the significance of this event. I had never in my Christian life been physically moved by the Spirit of God. I had heard of others having such experiences, but in the circles I moved in those experiences were always regarded with skepticism and were considered highly controversial. Now it had happened to me! There was no denying it. Nevertheless, I knew I was still very broken.

What I didn't perceive was that God was beginning to answer my prayer when I had fasted.

Later that week, Arthur, Derek and I were hanging out in front of the dorms when another student walked up to join the conversation. We noticed that this guy had a cast on his arm, so we asked him what had happened to his arm. He told us that he had gotten a stress fracture in his lower arm when he fell on it wrong while playing football. Having just had a dramatic encounter with God, our faith level was very high. Having been encouraged by Steve to pray for people to be healed, we were actually willing to try it. We then asked if we could pray for his arm. With a quick shrug he said, "Sure."

Arthur, Derek, and I began praying for this guy's arm. We stood there praying, "In Jesus name we speak to this arm, and we command it to be healed. Holy Spirit come!" Suddenly, we could see the guy's eyebrows raise.

He said, "Wow! I feel tingling inside my arm!"

We got very excited. When the tingling stopped, we presumed that God was done and that he was healed. Though there was no way to confirm it since he had a cast on, we all went away thrilled that God had given a physical confirmation to our prayer request.

On another night some of us were crossing the parking lot when we saw a man hobbling across the parking lot on crutches. He had just finished a night class and was getting ready to drive home. When we stopped to talk to him, we noticed that in addition to the crutches, he was wearing a splint on his ankle. We asked what had happened, and he went on to explain to us that he had fallen off a platform and had landed on the side of his foot. The result was a severe and painful injury. When we asked if we could lay hands on his foot and pray for it, there was no hint of hesitation. He just said, "That would be great!" We were standing near his truck, so with his driver door open, he sat sideways on the bench seat of his truck while we prayed. As soon as we laid hands on his foot and started praying, I felt a surge of power like electricity going through my hand. He obviously felt it as well because he got up before I could say anything and started to jump around the parking lot without crutches exclaiming, "I'm healed! I'm healed!" The splint was no longer needed.

We were all riding on cloud nine after these two events. As a matter of fact, we were so excited seeing God heal people that we started hunting for people to pray for. Our lack of experience and sensitivity quickly became evident. One day a pretty coed came up the stairs to the cafeteria. She had come for the evening meal when we all noticed a bandage around her knee. She noticed us all staring. In our zeal we offered to pray for her knee, practically falling over each other before she could even answer the question. As we converged on her simultaneously, she screamed and ran away!

From time to time I saw Tamba on campus at dorm devotions. This event would take place in either the men's or women's dorm lobby. Both had fireplaces, and in the cooler months a fire would be lit for atmosphere as the students would come together to worship. A message would often be given by a guest speaker or senior student. At other times I would see Tamba at convocation, held once a week in our chapel room on the other end of campus. On each occasion when I saw her, I had some kind of visceral reaction like my insides turning over. I would experience a jolt of fear, along with anxiety, pain, longing, regret, sorrow and abysmal emptiness, and trauma. I was still shell-shocked over the break up. This emotional reaction obviously exceeded the bounds of normal grief. However, I had determined to continue on. I would get through this. I would recover, even if it took forever. Believe me, I thought it *would* take forever! In spite of my troubles, I still had hope. My eyes were being opened to God's power. I was seeing God heal others, and I had every expectation that He would heal me as well.

CHAPTER 17

Eyes Wide Open

I THOUGHT I KNEW WHAT I was getting myself into. The end of the spring semester was upon us, and I would start my summer pastoral internship at Parkside Christian Church in Long Beach. My major in Diversified Ministries required me to complete a six-week pastoral internship. The church sponsoring me arranged for me to house sit for an older couple while they were away for the summer. I would have my own place, get to preach, serve with the youth, and do some house calls as well. I was very excited and couldn't wait to start. After packing my Mustang, I took off for Long Beach.

I later arrived at a very tiny church in the heart of the downtown area. The church rested on a corner with a postage-stamp-sized parking lot in back. It seemed to be in a rather depressed area, surrounded by residential, low-rent apartments. I also noticed a convalescent home directly across the street. At the church I was warmly greeted by Pastor Ramee and his wife who did their best to make me feel comfortable. They were a young, good-looking couple and seemed to be struggling to communicate something to me. They stood looking at me for a moment, and then they both looked at each other and then back at me. I knew right away that something was up.

Pastor Ramee spoke first. "Ah, we have a slight problem. It seems the couple that you were to house sit for will not be leaving on their vacation for a week or so. This means that until they leave we don't have a place for you to stay. So, we've had to make other arrangements. I hope you understand. Now the church owns a small place, a tiny parsonage, where you can stay while we are waiting for the McCarthys to leave on their vacation. Then you can house sit for them."

I was elated. "Well that seems great! So what seems to be the problem?"

The Pastor continued apologetically, "Well, you need to know that we are allowing a young man to stay in the house right now and that you'll need to share the....."

Mrs. Ramee interrupted, "The young man is homeless and the church is trying to help him kick drugs."

Pastor Ramee interjected, "He hasn't been sleeping well and seems to have some issues."

This raised my eyebrows, "Issues...what issues?" They again looked at each other as though searching for a way to explain the circumstances.

Pastor Ramee finally said, "He's been complaining that 'things' are interrupting his sleep." He illustrated with his fingers making quotation marks as he said it.

"What things?" I asked.

"Noises, mostly. I think he may have some mental problems or some psychological issues going on. We wanted you to know beforehand. He's a nice enough guy. Sincere. He's not violent or dangerous, or we wouldn't put you there. However, our options are limited right now," he explained apologetically.

"So what kinds of noises is he hearing?" I asked.

With a shrug of his shoulders, he said, "We really didn't get into a whole lot of that with him."

Finally, I asked, "So what is his name?"

"His name is Luis."

My curiosity had been piqued. After all my experiences in college last spring, my eyes had been opened to a much bigger reality. What I had read about and studied in the Scriptures, I was now experiencing firsthand. Consequently, I was much more reluctant to dismiss anything as being merely psychological. I gladly accepted the offer to room with Luis. Of course, at this point there was no other option.

When I met Luis, I was a little surprised. I was expecting someone a little less coherent. Luis, in contrast, was very clear, lucid, and even articulate. A man of dark complexion and average height, he explained to me that he had been living on the street for the last year or so and was trying to get off drugs. He said that he was mostly past the withdrawals and starting to feel a lot better. After moving my things into what I could only describe as a one-bedroom cottage, more of an apartment than a house, I talked with Luis a little more. As we talked further, I learned that Luis was having difficulty sleeping because of sounds in the night, and that *things* kept waking him up.

At this point I asked Luis if I could pray for him. He said, "Sure." I then put my hand on his back and began praying. As I prayed I could see his face starting to wince as though he were in extreme pain.

I asked, "What's wrong?"

"My lower back is knotting up! Feels like a Charlie horse!" He said it while holding his hand against the small of his back.

I then moved my hand down to where he indicated the knot was. As I did, the knot moved up his back into his shoulder and left him! I was stunned, shocked, and excited all at the same time. At that moment I thought there might be something more to Luis's nightly disturbances.

When I entered the parsonage there was a musty smell in the place. The air was stale. I moved my duffle, backpack and sleeping bag into the bedroom and settled in. That night started out as a fairly normal evening. We didn't have a TV, so we spent the early hours of the evening getting acquainted and talking about each other's prospective plans for the future. Luis talked about staying clean (off drugs), finding full-time work and finding a room for rent. I talked about my desire to get into full-time ministry and to possibly pastor my own church someday. As the night wore on, it started to get late. We were both tired, so we settled in for some much needed shut-eye.

What followed that evening was something I had never before experienced in my life, nor have I since. We had just turned the lights out and were bedding down in our sleeping bags because there were no beds. No sooner had we started trying to sleep, when we heard a clear TAP, TAP on the wall to the left side of the room. It was a sound that I normally would have ignored. I would have regarded the sound as the house settling, or maybe old wood studs expanding or contracting because of temperature changes in the wall, except that I was now sensitized to my surroundings, having been exposed to some extraordinary things in college. Also, my briefing by the pastor on Luis's history, together with his physical reaction to my prayer, made me even more sensitized than I would normally be.

Staring up at the ceiling in the dark, I asked Luis, "Is that what you were talking about Luis?"

"Yeah...that's it."

I didn't think much of it. "Luis, it's likely the house settling." Immediately after I said that, there were three, loud, deliberate taps on the wall again.

"That's not the house settling!" Luis asserted.

"You have got to be kidding me!" I got up and quickly turned on the lights. I placed my hand on the door knob. A sudden fear came over me, as though I had just walked into an invisible cloud of foreboding. The hair on the back of my neck began to prickle. My heart was pounding in my chest. Slowly, I opened the bedroom door and walked into the next room to see if by chance it might be something explainable. The faint wail of a siren sounded somewhere in the distance. *Maybe it's a cicada banging it's head against the wall.* I slowly checked the next room and quickly dismissed the cicada theory realizing that Long Beach was a major metropolitan area and didn't have cicadas. I then came back into the bedroom. For a moment we stared out at the open bedroom door into the dark gloom of the tiny living room. I closed the door, turning the light off again, and returned to my sleeping bag on the floor. The white panel door just stood there like a ghost in the darkness.

Suddenly, there were several loud taps coming from the wall on the right side of the room: loud, sharp, distinct! *This can't be really happening.*

I'm still not quite believing what I think is going on. I'm trying to process and interpret what's happening as the hairs on the back of my neck continue to stand up. My mind is grappling with the awareness that we are obviously not alone. Something lay beyond the shadows of this tiny hovel, something sinister. But what? I'm still not sure what I'm dealing with.

I figured, *What have I got to lose?* So while still lying down, I rebuked this noise. "In the name of Jesus, go! Leave!" Whatever it was must have taken my rebuke as a challenge because a chorus of tapping noises erupted off all four walls. Luis and I were beside ourselves. I'm still thinking, *This can't be happening. Nobody's going to believe this!*

I stood up, turned on the light, and proceeded to rebuke these noises once again. "In the name of Jesus Christ, I command you to stop and go away!" The tapping stopped momentarily and then started up again shortly afterwards. At this point I didn't know what to do. My commands were going unheeded. Our hearts were racing, and fear gripped us.

Now the tapping sounds were coming from all directions simultaneously, including the ceiling, loud and clear. There was no mistaking these noises to be by chance or anything other than what they were. The sounds persisted, and we continued being harassed by these unseen tormentors. Then, after what seemed like a very long time, the sounds slowed down and almost stopped altogether. We waited. My adrenaline had kicked in, and my pulse was racing. I was incredulous. I was on high alert. Luis and I were both tensed up with our eyes wide. And there we stood in the dim glow of the room on guard, not knowing what to do.

Then there was a sudden loud knock on the bedroom door! Three deliberate, heavy, clear knocks! Startled to think that someone else was in the house, I immediately walked over to the door and opened it. Nobody was there, just the dim light cast from the bedroom swallowed up by the darkness of the empty living room. *This has got to be a joke, right?* Even as I'm thinking it, I'm getting creeped out. I turned to Luis, and his face had gone pale. He was just as alarmed as I was. He was visibly disturbed. "Is anybody else staying here Luis?" I asked, already knowing the answer to my own question.

Without hesitation he said, "No...Nobody's stayin' here 'cept us."

We then walked through the small dwelling and turned on all the lights in every room. This exercise took next to no time at all because of the shelter's small size. After finding nobody there, the creep factor increased significantly for me. I starting thinking, *What the blazes have I gotten myself into? Nobody is going to believe this. I wouldn't believe this if it wasn't happening right in front of me!* Thumbing over my shoulder at the door, I asked Luis, "Has *that* happened before?"

"No. The knock never happened before." He said as he stood there wringing his hands.

The sounds seemed to stop momentarily. We eventually turned the lights out and settled back down again. Then we were alarmed again by more strange phenomena a few minutes later. What we then began to hear I can only describe as the sound of footsteps in the short hallway (like dress shoes on linoleum) and again, with no one visibly there, occasional scratching noises in the walls and ceiling. The tapping continued intermittently.

Then, in a moment of silence, an audible growl came from the attic. This wasn't an animal type of growl. It sounded far more sinister, otherworldly, and even human-like. Luis and I immediately looked at each other, eyes wide, to confirm that we were both hearing the same thing. We were even being kept awake by sudden movement inside our sleeping bags. It was terrifying, like something right out of a dark, horror movie. I couldn't believe what I was experiencing.

Into the late evening and early morning hours I would, time and again, rebuke these entities, and each time it was to no avail. With our skin crawling and our hair standing on end, I knew that we were dealing with evil spirits and that these manifestations were demonic. As a Bible-believing Christian, I continued to deal with the situation the only way I knew how.

I spoke out loud repeatedly saying, "In the name of Jesus Christ, I command you to stop! I command you to go! Now! Leave, in Jesus' name!" Again, the tapping would stop momentarily, only to start up again the next moment. Later, the tapping became intermittent but continued to emanate from all four walls and the ceiling. Each time, with the most assertive voice I could muster, I rebuked these entities. I repeated myself again and again but without effect. It was as though we were being mocked by some unseen, evil presence. Fear clung to us, and the harassment went on. Throughout that night we continued to be harassed by loud knocks on the bedroom door and repeated tapping on the ceiling and walls.

Here I was, an intern pastor, and I was completely ineffective in handling this situation. As a Christian, I knew that Jesus was greater in power and authority. I also knew that demons had to bow to Jesus' name, and yet I felt powerless to do anything about what was happening.

What I didn't know then, and what I wouldn't come to know until much later, was that I had committed sins in my past that had opened doorways into my life that had given access to evil and the right to occupy. These doorways involved violence, pornography, lust, and a foolish, one-time experiment with a Ouija board as a kid. These sins, along with my own fragmented soul, had opened doorways and given access to these demonic spirits. I knew nothing about such things at the time. These previous agreements (sins) needed to be renounced, but because I was unaware of this necessity, I was at a loss as to what I could do about it. The torment continued. Needless to say, we didn't get a lot of sleep that night.

The following day I was still stunned and shocked as I reflected on what had happened the previous night. My eyes were being opened; I had once again been made aware of another whole new reality. I knew that Jesus was more powerful than any demon, yet my commands were being ignored and unheeded. I was confident that God was all-powerful and still in absolute control. I concluded, therefore, that there had to be another explanation as to why I was so ineffective.

The worst thing for me was feeling like I couldn't confide in the senior pastor. After all, he had already suggested that Luis might have some mental problems, or "issues," as he called them. I didn't want him looking at me like I was some nut-job. But what was I going to say? *"Oh, by the way Pastor Ramee, you have an infestation of demons in your parsonage!"* Yeah, that would go over well! I could just hear him now, *"Well David, the elders and I just had a meeting, and we've decided that our church is really not suited for an intern program. We think you would be better served at a larger church with more resources."*

I decided not to tell the pastor. He would never believe it. *I* probably wouldn't have believed it if it had not happened right in front of me. It was all very fantastic, difficult to explain, and controversial. I was very conflicted. On the one hand, I thought the pastor should know what's going on, but on the other hand, I could tell that he was clearly not ready to hear about something like this. The fact of the matter was, my life had just been catapulted into a whole new reality. I was undergoing a paradigm shift and a rapid change in my worldview. I had been given new eyes. I was all of a sudden seeing the world through a completely different lens, and I was still running to catch up. What I soon discovered was that many Christians believed in angels and demons and healing in theory, but not in reality. Not here. Not today, and not now. Not in our modern world.

Pastor Ramee was a seminary graduate with a master's degree in divinity. This man, like many evangelical clergy that I knew, was very cerebral and rationalistic in his understanding and theology. I came close a couple of times to broaching the subject of the supernatural but thought better of it. I quickly realized in our dialogue that the man had no grid or filter for receiving my account of the recent events in the parsonage. I held my tongue. Over the course of that week, I began to become accustomed to the manifestations. I began to perceive them as a nuisance rather than any real threat. That perception turned out to be wrong.

That week Luis was at a bus stop going for a job interview when he was attacked by a man and punched several times. He was so angry and discouraged that he nearly went back to using drugs. After our experiences at the parsonage, I was beginning to interpret all my circumstances through a prism of supernatural influence. Consequently, I understood this attack to be retaliation against Luis for trying to get free from addiction. I perceived Luis's attacker to be under demonic influence, sent by the enemy to discourage Luis's progress to stay sober. Luis and I discussed this possibility at some length, and he reached the same conclusion. This realization kept him from giving up. In the end we were feeling like two embattled soldiers in a foxhole. Luis did what most rational people would do and found another place to live. I stayed, knowing that the McCarthys were leaving for their vacation soon. I anticipated moving out of the parsonage and spending time alone with God and having some peace of mind.

At this time, Pastor Ramee took me along to call on a lady whose husband was on his death bed. We were going there to pray with them and comfort the family. Having seen God heal a number of people the previous spring, I was sure that God was going to raise this guy from his death bed. I thought, *this is going to be a phenomenal miracle!* My faith was high because of what I had seen God do at the college, so I really believed God was going to heal this man. When we got there, we entered a very comfortable looking home with wood paneling. The walls and the decor were dark, masculine, but warm-looking. The Gradys had been long-standing members of the church and had some history with the pastor. Their older daughter was present, and both mother and daughter seemed to be comforting one another. Mrs. Grady brought us into what must have been the downstairs den before it had been made into a makeshift bedroom with a hospital bed. When we came in, Mr. Grady was not responsive, and I could tell that his breathing was labored.

Pastor Ramee and I both stood at the bedside of Mr. Grady, a twenty-three year member of Parkside Christian Church. He seemed unaware that we were even in the room. Mrs. Grady left us to pray for him and joined her daughter in the living room. When the door closed I said, "If you don't mind, I'd like to pray for him." The pastor, gesturing with his hand, gave me a look as if to say *go right ahead.* So, I gently put my hand on Mr. Grady, being careful to not put any weight on his chest, and began to pray.

"Father God, I thank you for your power, anointing, and your healing touch. I invite you to come, Holy Spirit, and I ask you to release your healing now in Jesus' name! I speak to the sickness afflicting this man's body, and in the name of Jesus, I command you to go! I speak to this man's body, and I command it to be healed in Jesus' name!"

At that point I began to feel heat in my hands. Then Mr. Grady started to make a gurgling sound in his throat. I brightened up thinking God was healing him. Then he was gone. Mr. Grady died. He passed away right in front of me! Disappointment washed over me as I realized that I had missed what I believed God was doing. I was sure God would heal him, and now it was too late. After informing the family, we stayed a while longer with Mrs. Grady and her daughter. I noticed a thick presence of God's peace, much like when Steve led worship back at the college. Once we felt the time was right, we left.

On the way back to the church, I said to Pastor Ramee, half disappointed and half apologizing, "I really thought that God was going to heal him."

Driving, he glanced sideways at me and said, "God did heal him!" I gave him a quizzical look.

"No more death, sorrow, or pain," he clarified.

Then the thought occurred to me. *Maybe God had wanted me to mid-wife this guy into heaven! After all, he had been in that condition for weeks. What were the odds that he would die right after my prayer?* I was mildly encouraged that God might have used me in such a way, but it was probably a testimony I would keep to myself.

CHAPTER 18

When All Heaven Breaks Loose

THIS WAS TURNING OUT TO be the strangest year of my life, and it was only getting stranger as time went on. Naturally, I was ecstatic to leave the parsonage for the McCarthy's house. Mrs. McCarthy had set out clean sheets in the master bedroom before leaving. Their townhouse had a small living room and a tiny kitchen with a breakfast bar. To the right of the kitchen was a short hallway with a bathroom on the left and a smaller bedroom on the right. At the end of the hallway was the master bedroom with its own bathroom. The whole place smelled like potpourri and scented candles, reminding me of a Hallmark store. The change was a relief.

I only had a duffle bag full of clothes and a backpack, so it didn't take me long to settle in. It had been a long week of ministry, and I hadn't slept much. I was really looking forward to having time alone and getting some rest and relaxation. I showered that night and put on some loose clothing. There was a big, comfortable, leather recliner in the living room, and a small round cherrywood table with a reading lamp on it. I stood there in glee thinking, *This is just perfect!* I nestled into the chair looking forward to reading a book. I had not stopped moving since arriving in Long Beach. I had literally been on the go since day one. It was nice to finally relax.

I had been reading for about fifteen minutes when my torso and shoulders began to slowly bob and move back and forth involuntarily like a buoy in the ocean. It was just like my experience last spring in the classroom with Steve and the group. Something had entered the room, and it felt like a thick blanket of peace. God was present. I realized that God was stirring me. I immediately put my book down and sat down on the floor with my legs crossed as I did before. Then I started to ask God for more. (Something I had heard Steve pray from time to time.) "More, Lord! More, Lord!" I felt a slight tingle through my body. I prayed. "More of whatever it is you're giving me!" The power began to increase. I continued to repeat myself, thanking Him and asking Him for more. "More, Lord!" Each time I asked for more, He came stronger and stronger. The power increased. I was filled with pure joy, and I couldn't contain myself. Laughter poured out of me. "Thank you Lord! More Lord!" As I asked Him for more, His power increased even more! Now He came even stronger as jolts of raw power began coursing through my body. My body started to convulse as the surges of power increased at my every request. Now every cell in my body was alive and on fire, and I thought that my body would explode at any moment! Yet I kept asking for more! Then all heaven broke loose. The increase came as my body went into involuntary spasms under the power. I could no longer stay in a sitting position as my body kept bouncing two feet off the floor! At one point it literally felt like ten thousand volts were going through my body! I was completely overwhelmed, excited and giddy! I had never experienced anything like this in my life, and I'd never felt more alive!

When I looked at the clock, I realized that I had spent the last four hours in prayer, yet the time went by as minutes! That night I hardly slept as my body kept convulsing under the power, and though I had hardly slept, I was completely refreshed the next morning. In the nights that followed, God's power continued to come. It was as though he had ordained this period of time just to be with me. It was the most incredible season of my life. I would serve all day at church performing various ministry tasks, only looking forward to getting back to my place where I could be alone with God and experience His presence again at the end of the day. The visitations continued for some time, and I often spent all night talking to Him, even choosing not to sleep. It was an amazing period of time.

Toward the last week of summer, I had a sense that God was bringing me into a new season, a season of *house cleaning*. What I didn't quite comprehend was that my unusual encounter with God's power was a sovereign act on His part to break loose some things from my life. Generational spirits and other demonic strongholds were just some of the things He wanted me to face and deal with, things like rejection, fear, lust, and abandonment. God was forcing me to deal with my demons (literally), and the real battle was just beginning.

This became more obvious as I approached my last week of summer. The power surges had stopped. Now I was beginning to have some very different experiences that I knew were not God at all. The demons that had plagued Luis and me at the parsonage were now starting to harass me at the townhouse. Even beyond my previous experiences, bizarre manifestations were starting to occur at the townhouse and were even worse than before. For example, when I tried to sleep, my bed would shake. On several occasions the doorknob to my bedroom spontaneously turned making a "shick-shick" sound. On other occasions I felt something making depressions on my bed like an animal walking up on me. I was experiencing sudden movements under my bed sheets again with nothing visibly there. Sometimes I would go into the kitchen to find the water running. I would turn it off only to come back later and find it running again. This went on through the last week of my summer internship.

One day it finally dawned on me. I had a revelation that the demons were not attached to the parsonage or to the place I was staying at, but to *me personally!* The demons were attached to *me*, not the place! That revelation came to me when I was at the church one night doing some paperwork. It was still early in the evening. The church was empty, the staff having gone home for the day, and I was alone. I thought. The place was dark and quiet with the exception of my office where I had my desk lamp on. I went briefly to another room to get a stapler. When I came back, I was standing by my desk when I was suddenly kicked very hard from behind. It felt as if I had been kicked by someone wearing a hard shoe. It was a painful kick with lots of force behind it, and I reacted instantly! I spun around to unload my wrath on the person standing there. Nobody was there! No one! Nada! That is when it dawned on me how serious my situation was. This attack began to wake me up to the inherent danger threatening me.

I immediately began to panic. Up to this point, I had never been physically harmed by these entities. But now things were escalating. I knew right then that I needed immediate help. At that moment, seized by an overwhelming sense of urgency, I considered my options. I couldn't go to the pastor. He was completely in the dark about all this stuff. Besides, the Ramees would've completely freaked out if I told them, or they would've rationalized a mental breakdown by their intern. For Pete's sake, *I* was freaking out! I just couldn't go back to the townhouse. I didn't want to be alone. With no one to turn to, and nowhere else to go, I decided to go to the Harvest Crusade being held at the Anaheim Stadium. I had heard about the event earlier and decided not to go, but my circumstances were dire now. I jumped in my car and drove all the way to Anaheim that same evening.

When I pulled into the parking lot of Anaheim Stadium, the event was already in full swing. I found parking with very little effort and walked in with the rest of the late stragglers. I walked quickly up the ramps smelling food from the concessions and listening to the booming of the speakers in the background. I walked out of one of the tunnels into the open crowd and quickly found a seat. I knew the event was primarily for reaching unbelievers, but I didn't care. I just needed someone to pray for me. I was desperately anticipating the invitation. As soon as they gave the invitation, I started to make my way down to the ballfield, repenting every step of the way. I went forward repenting of every sin I could think of. I knew that I was battling with lust and would struggle to sleep at night, but I hadn't realized that I was in bondage. I confessed to God and repented. When I arrived down at the baseball diamond, a young man greeted me and prayed with me. I realized now that I had become accustomed to these demonic manifestations. I had become complacent, seduced. My mind had become fogged, my thinking clouded. My eyes had been blinded to how this demonic activity was escalating into something very dangerous. Through the crusade, God brought me to a place of realization and repentance.

That night God took off the blinders and opened my eyes to the truth. Ironically, these creepy manifestations had forced me to seek much-needed help. I later drove back to Long Beach with a full understanding of what I was dealing with. I was declaring war on the demonic, and I had determined to take no prisoners. I would resist the devil at every turn. I would rebuke these entities as often as I needed to. I would not allow myself to settle or get complacent again.

When I got back to the townhouse, I was at peace, but determined. I first started praying, pleading the blood of Jesus over myself and over every room in the house especially the bedroom. When a spirit would begin to manifest, I would shout it down in Jesus' name. My new disposition toward these manifestations and the renewed condition of my heart seemed to make a difference. Formerly, I was unaware of my bondage or the seriousness of my condition. Now I was fully aware and determined to get free. That night I slept better, but I was not out of the woods yet.

I was one week away from the start of the fall semester, and I couldn't wait to talk to Steve Hampton. He would certainly know what to do about my situation. I battled through that week, hardly sleeping at times. Though the demonic activity seemed a little more subdued than before, I was still being tormented. Something had shifted. There was a wrinkle in the natural order of things. A door had been opened that had changed my world, and I couldn't get back. Nothing seemed *normal* anymore. Somewhere along the way I had broken a sacred law in the universe. I had crossed a line. I had opened a portal to the unknown. I was being harassed by demons. My sleep continued to be broken. It was the end of my internship, and I had one week of summer left before classes would begin. I needed to get free from my torment, but I didn't have the slightest idea where to begin. I needed to find Steve Hampton.

PART III

A Journey of
Transformation

CHAPTER 19

Planet Meltdown

WHEN THE FALL SEMESTER STARTED, I was feeling a lot like "Buffy the Vampire Slayer" In this tongue-in-cheek B movie, Buffy (played by Kristy Swanson) is a carefree cheerleader, preoccupied with the usual extra-curricular activities of high school adolescents. One day she is accosted by a dark and mysterious man (played by Donald Sutherland) and informed that she is "The Chosen One," called to battle the forces of evil. Perceiving this guy to be a creepy nut-job, she ignores the prophetic call as mere quackery, until one day she is forced to defend herself against an onslaught of attack by these dark forces. Awakened to the reality that vampires *do* exist, she is shaken from her trite, adolescent existence. With her eyes wide open, she undergoes a major paradigm shift. No longer able to indulge her friends in their glib, superficial pettiness, Buffy undergoes a serious transformation as she realizes that everything she was told by the man was, in fact, true. Embracing her destiny, she finally becomes who she was always called to be from the beginning... the next vampire slayer.

My comparison breaks down quickly as a very loose identification with this movie. However, the scene in which Buffy returns to school after her *awakening* aptly summarizes what I felt returning to college. There I stood in the middle of the campus watching students walk by, enroute to wherever it was they needed to be. I felt compelled to warn all these innocent young students about what had happened to me! I wanted them all to know what I had experienced and discovered. I now knew demons were REAL, with a capital R! Yet, I couldn't say anything about it without looking like a crackpot. I wanted to yell at the top of my lungs, "Hey everybody! The sky is falling!" But I knew that I would have about as much credibility as Chicken Little himself. Instead, I just kept quiet and looked for Steve Hampton.

When I finally found Steve, I immediately launched into my story. With wide eyes and demonstrative hand motions, I told him all about what I had experienced that summer. He just stood there, arms crossed, nodding acknowledgement to my words, listening patiently to my tireless monologue about my discovery of Satan's demonic plot against me and the world. Finally, out of breath, I fell silent. Steve looked off in the distance for a moment, then back at me, and said, "Come with me to the Vineyard." I decided that I would go to the next service being held.

The Vineyard was a large church in Anaheim. At that time they were in the middle of renovating a large building they had purchased, so they were meeting in a big circus tent. Vineyard Christian Fellowship of Anaheim was like no other church I had ever been to or experienced up to that point. When Steve and I got there, we sat to the left of the stage. Steve was greeted by a number of people with whom he seemed to share a history. I noticed one particular couple sitting behind and to the left of us. I noticed them because they stood out from all the glowing faces around them. The couple looked very gaunt, like death-warmed-over. They were ghostly pale with dark circles under their eyes. Both were stoic looking and expressionless.

The worship music was amazing, rapturous and went on for quite some time. The crowd stood with arms raised toward heaven. The atmosphere was permeated with excitement and expectation, but the pale couple behind us remained unresponsive. When the worship ended, a heavyset man with white hair and a matching beard stepped out from behind the keyboards. The crowd intuitively sat down. The man stepped up to the pulpit and began to teach in a very conversational tone. I later learned that this man was Pastor John Wimber. When he finished, he said he sensed God wanting to minister and invited anyone who needed healing to stand up. I turned around to see the pale couple behind us standing. A number of other people also stood to receive prayer that night. As they stood, Pastor Wimber told the people sitting near them to lay hands on them and begin praying for them. I could see several people praying for this pale couple, including Steve. The prayer went on for quite some time. When this ministry time was finally over, the pale couple were both soaked with sweat and color had returned to their faces. They were even *smiling*, something I hadn't seen them do since they walked in. They had been visibly set free from some kind of bondage. That was the first of many amazing things I would witness at this gathering. Word soon reached our college group of all that God was doing there, and our whole group came to check it out.

We all began attending the Vineyard's services. The worship seemed magical, anointed. The atmosphere was electric and full of faith. I noticed right away that every time I went to a service, I would leave feeling very emotional, like a big sob was just brewing inside my chest. I was still feeling brokenhearted over Tamba, and God was helping me deal with that loss. For example, on more than one occasion, when I was singing, I started crying spontaneously. As the worship continued, tears streamed down my cheeks. When my nose started to run, I noticed boxes of tissue under every few seats as though the church was expecting this kind of thing to occur. At first, I felt *very* self-conscious and embarrassed as my broken heart would spontaneously erupt in a flood of tears. *I'm melting down in front of everybody! What's happening to me? Public displays of emotion are just never cool!* However, when I noticed a lot of other hurting people around me, I got over myself. It was evident that God was touching and healing people all over the place in this church.

When I returned to the college that night, I was reeling from the whole experience. Our college group continued attending the Vineyard and meeting together on campus. Within a few weeks the Vineyard church moved out of the tent and into the new building. A month later the church hosted a healing conference and our whole group made a point to attend.

The healing conference was amazing! Steve Hampton, Arthur, Tim, Derek, Karen, Todd, and Steve Burger all attended. When we came into the new Vineyard facility, we entered a huge lobby that divided into two tunnels. These tunnels led into a very large, carpeted sanctuary with graduated, theater seating that held about three thousand people. Large screens flanked both sides of a very large stage. Women danced, whirling banners and waving flags as they worshipped to rock rhythm praise. We were amazed as we heard and witnessed visiting pastors and prophets give words and prophecies to individuals with pinpoint accuracy. Numerous healings and miracles resulted. Pastor John Wimber opened the meeting with a message about the Father-Heart of God. At the end of the message Wimber said, "Holy Spirit, come!" At that moment, I felt what I can only describe as a thick cloud descending in the room. Many fell to the floor. I had to hold onto the back of the seat in front of me to keep from falling because my head was getting so light. Trained ministry team members began to go around the room laying hands on people and praying for them.

The conference was three days long with two sessions per day and a number of workshops. I have always been a highly social person, typically hanging out with friends after such events. God, however, had other plans. I experienced a meltdown after every session of the conference. Literally after every invitation, I found myself at the front steps of the altar sobbing, red-nosed and puffy-eyed. I became a permanent fixture there. Everything seemed perfectly tailored for me, and God wasn't leaving me alone for a minute.

As the ministry team members prayed for me, God did His first miracle in my life. He healed me of shame. Shame, I learned, is self-rejection. My soul was fragmented. God showed me that I had rejected part of my self, the child part. It was that child part that made me vulnerable to others. Since it had never been safe to be vulnerable, I walled that inner-child off. The result was that I had become limited in my ability to experience and express emotion. My breakup with Tamba only hindered my emotions more.

As the ministry team prayed for me, God reached down into my past and brought forth a memory. In my mind's eye I saw myself as a ten-year-old child huddled in a corner alone, crying. I was then encouraged to reconcile with my inner-child. The ministry team coached me to approach this child, who was me. I asked the child to forgive me for rejecting him and pushing him away. This inner child forgave me, and we embraced each other. As we did so, a flood of tears came as I once again identified with this young boy and all the pain he went through. Then Jesus appeared in the memory. With one hand on my shoulder and the other on this little boy, He merged us back together as one. This all took place in my mind's eye as a memory. It was a miracle that had an immediate and profound impact on my life.

When I came out of it, I began to experience a sense of peace and soundness that I had never had before. It was a peace that went straight to my bones. I was different, and I knew it. The following week I was getting ready for Homiletics class when I looked into the bathroom mirror and noticed that the light had returned to my eyes! I stood there mesmerized, staring at the obvious difference in my countenance. It was a visible sign that God had given back to me something that I never could have recovered on my own. It was a miracle. I now had restored to me a degree of wholeness. That was just the first of many miracles God started to do.

That healing conference kicked off a whole series of other miracles and started a spiritual domino effect in my life that year.

CHAPTER 20

Strange Occurrences

OUR LITTLE BAND OF BELIEVERS started to experience God's power in amazing ways that year. Not only did God begin healing our hearts individually, but he started healing and delivering others through us. Because this was a conservative evangelical Christian college, signs and wonders were not the norm. Consequently, word started getting back to the faculty that some strange occurrences were taking place on campus.

The first of these strange occurrences was a man getting delivered from demons as we prayed for him late one night outside the school library. Loud, unnatural wails pierced the darkness of the night at the far end of campus as we sought to get this individual free from demons. This was disturbing and shook up some of the student body. We tried to seek out more discrete places, but that proved to be difficult.

On another occasion a young girl was wheeled by her boyfriend into the dorm lobby in a wheelchair. She seemed very limited in her movement. She was fair-skinned with wavy, brown hair, wide-rimmed glasses, and wore a serious expression on her face. We asked about her condition, and she told us that she had leukemia. We explained that this disease was no different from a common cold to God, and that He could heal her easily. Our faith was high, and our confidence knew no bounds. When we asked if we could pray and lay hands on her, she said, "Yes." When we laid hands on her, I said, "Holy Spirit, come!" The power of God started low, but I could tell by the surprised look on her face that she could feel it. I said, "More, Lord!" The power increased suddenly and shot though her body like an electric current! Her body started shaking under the power, and she was laughing uncontrollably as I kept praying, "More, Holy Spirit! Heal her, God!" When we stopped praying, she got up and started dancing around, feeling very giddy. Then she and her boyfriend, who had been pushing her, left pushing an empty wheelchair! We were flying high at that moment!

I had figured that her healing was a done deal. We had not yet learned about spiritual opposition to healing and the need to battle doubt and stand in faith for healing. Later, I was disappointed to learn that this girl still struggled with her illness. We continued to pray for her full recovery. I would later discover the need to declare and decree God's word over a condition and to stand on His promises until they come to pass.

On still another evening, we helped another student get free from a demon. In the dormitory there are two floors of dorm rooms with a common area and study hall between the two wings. Above that common area was a small, third story loft that we would often go to for prayer. We had taken a young man there for deliverance. The deliverance was so loud that it was disturbing and freaking out some of the students who were trying to study in the lower tiers of the building.

These kinds of strange occurrences started getting reported back to the faculty. Consequently, my friends and I eventually got called into the office of one of the professors. This summons gave me a strange feeling that trouble was looming on the horizon, and that we had somehow stepped over the line. When I learned that we were meeting with Professor Allen Ferrell (the husband of Mrs. Ferrell, who had saved me from Mr. Montgomery's World Civ. Class) I was somewhat relieved. I surmised that he must have lost the coin toss to be the one speaking to us. I soon learned that was not the case.

Professor Allen Ferrell was Mrs. Elaine Ferrell's husband and also a faculty member. Mr. Ferrell wore a sweater, casual slacks, and was basically the opposite of Mrs. Ferrell in personality. He was a tall, genteel man with blond, curly hair and blue eyes. All the students liked him for his wisdom and understanding. Everyone knew him to have a genuine love for the students. When we arrived at Professor Ferrell's office, he asked us if we would like to have a seat. Arthur, Derek and I all sat down without answering. He casually walked over and closed the door for privacy.

"Gentlemen, I appreciate your time. I wanted to speak to you privately to make you all aware that some of the students have recently expressed concerns to the faculty regarding some of your activity on campus."

We all looked at each other. I leaned forward in my chair. "Activity... what activity specifically, Mr. Ferrell?"

The professor was a calm and patient man, which was probably the reason he was chosen to speak with us.

"Specifically some of the students are complaining, saying that you were...ah...casting out *demons* in the dormitory. Ring any bells?"

We shifted in our seats, about to explain, when he continued, "laying hands on people, praying for arms and legs to be healed." He paused, looked at us silently, smiling, and then continued, "Praying is good, and these are all good things you are doing."

He then stood up, came around the front of his desk, and sat on the edge. Leaning forward and looking us each in the eye, he lowered his voice as though leery of imaginary eavesdroppers or spies and said, "Between us, I know you are excited and zealous about this stuff, and I am all for what you are doing. It sounds like God is doing some amazing things on campus. We probably even share the same theology. I just want to encourage you to be a little more sensitive to the other students who may not be in the same place you are. Please try to exercise a little discretion regarding other people around you. Ok? Any questions?"

We all sat there amazed that we were actually receiving encouragement and support instead of a reprimand. We all started in at once, excited and sharing our different stories of what God had done on campus. Shutting his eyes, Mr. Ferrell held up his index finger, "One at a time, gentlemen."

We left Professor Ferrell's office feeling affirmed by an ally. It was a great feeling, and I was riding high. That semester I managed to keep myself occupied between classes, homework, and friends. I stayed busy enough to keep Tamba from the forefront of my mind. However, as I was walking briskly from class one day, there she was again with *that guy*. They were standing at the end of the walkway, talking in the parking lot. *Great!...I'm going to have to walk past them. Do I say hi? Do I ignore them? For Pete's sake, David, act your age. Say "hi." Introduce yourself—be mature.*

I got to the end of the walkway and realized that I couldn't do it. I just couldn't be mature. I wasn't ready for this. *I know, I'll just give a quick wave on the way by.* So, I waved.

Tamba made eye contact and said, "Hi."

Those eyes....they suck me in every time. Before I could think, I stopped and said, "Hi Tamba." Then I stepped off the curb and approached them. *What the heck am I doing?* Before I realized what I was doing, I was reaching out shaking hands with this guy. The corner of his mouth was sneering at me slightly.

I just grimaced. "I guess we're brothers whether we like it or not," I said. He didn't have a comeback for that. Tamba gave a nervous laugh.

Then I said, "See you later."

I could have interpreted this event as a victory, but I felt discouraged. When I got back to my dorm room, I sat on my bed reflecting, hurting, deflated, and somber. How could I be on the mountaintop one minute and then back down to the pit the next? It was exasperating.

Later, after getting out of class, I ran into Arthur and Derek. They could see something was wrong and offered to pray for me. I accepted. They stopped and prayed heartfelt prayers for me right there in the hallway as students walked past on their way to class. I was really appreciating the friends they'd become. They were becoming more like family to me as the relationships in our group deepened over time. God was working through these relationships to help me get truly free from the bondage of my past.

CHAPTER 21

Breaking Free

IN MY JUNIOR YEAR OF college I was still experiencing a long season of deliverance. I was still not completely free from my past and the lies that had bound me. I was still experiencing harassment by demonic spirits, and I often had to anoint my forehead at night with oil, pleading the blood of Jesus over myself before going to bed. I was also playing worship music all night, on a loop, at a very low volume to avoid disturbing my roommates. These practices served to suppress the manifestations, allowing me to sleep. One by one, demonic doorways were being closed, but I still was not out of the woods yet.

I started attending the Vineyard's Small Ministry Team and meeting with some people who specialized in deliverance ministry. These individuals were very well trained and skilled in discerning spirits. They also demonstrated a lot of spiritual authority when praying. This was very comprehensive prayer ministry, and my deepest darkest secrets were laid bare. I didn't care, though. I was desperate to be completely free at any cost. I just wanted my life back. I wanted to be able to enjoy and experience a *normal* healthy life with normal, healthy relationships.

As I attended these sessions, I was delivered from a number of demons (familiar spirits) that had attached themselves to me when spiritual doorways were opened through violence, trauma, pornography, and the Ouija board I had played with once as a child. There were a number of agreements with the enemy and inner vows that I had made without realizing it. These sins, agreements, and vows had given demonic spirits the right to occupy.

Once I had confessed and renounced my past sins, vows, and agreements, I asked God to cover these with the blood of Jesus. Then I received His forgiveness and cleansing by faith. Jesus' blood and sacrifice paid for, washed away, and blotted out all my sin and stain, so the demons no longer had any rights or grounds to torment me. At that moment I was declared forgiven, and these afflicting spirits were commanded to leave me. I was delivered from spirits of violence, trauma, pornography, lust, and poverty, as well as a religious spirit.

I was also set free from a number of generational curses handed down to me through my family bloodline. These included generational alcoholism and addiction as well as divorce and poverty. These curses were typically perpetuated by a demon or demons that would continue to enforce the curse. However, though I was free, that wasn't the end of it. The enemy doesn't give up ground easily. Even God's chosen people in the Bible could only enter their promised land through battle. I needed to learn how to stand my ground and fight, not only to get free but to stay free. I began to learn how to stand in my faith by renouncing the lies I had believed and by declaring God's truth in their place. This truth I spoke out loud with conviction.

There was eventually some demonic retaliation for evicting these evil spirits from my life. This season of retaliation would manifest itself as an irrational fear. One night I was being continually threatened, not by any audible voice, but by a thought in my head, a thought that wouldn't go away. This demonic threat came as a powerful lie saying that if I were to leave the dorms that night for any reason, I would be killed.

The fear came over me with an indescribable intensity. The thought was so powerful and convincing that I really believed harm would come to me if I left the dorms for any reason. I knew the thought was completely irrational. After all, I was living on the campus of a Christian college; I couldn't imagine a safer place to be. For that reason I knew the threats were demonic in origin. However, I also knew that the demons were real. I hadn't yet come to fully understand spiritual authority.

It was my dear brother Arthur who stood vigil with me up in the loft of the dormitory, praying. It was a long dark night, and we were up for hours. Arthur faithfully encouraged me. Eventually we succumbed to fatigue and fell asleep. In the morning when the sunlight was streaming through the windows, that sense of impending doom had finally abated. Arthur's presence and prayer helped me get through a very dark and difficult season while getting free. Arthur's friendship was invaluable, and I couldn't have been more grateful.

One afternoon in my junior year of college, Tim rallied some of us guys together and suggested we form a men's group. He suggested we commit to meeting together as a quorum once a week for a year. He knew that each of us dealt with different issues and that we could each benefit from mutual accountability and mentorship.

Tim asked us as a group and then individually, looking at each of us in the eye, "Will you commit to one year? Will you do that?"

We all readily agreed, and from that point on we started meeting together. The group included Tim Gray, Arthur Andrews, Steve Burger and me. We met once a week for a year in different places. Sometimes it was out on the campus on the grassy area. Sometimes it was in the dorms. Sometimes we would all go to Naugle Burgers for a coke and fries and sit in a booth and talk. At other times we would meet at the snack bar or in the library. Together, each of us checked in with the group. We shared our struggles, failures, and our victories. We spoke affirmation and encouragement to each other. When necessary, we corrected one another. Of course we always prayed, and the prayer had a powerful impact on all of us.

It wouldn't be until later that I would realize the profound impact that this men's group had on me. We all received some level of healing and restoration as we gave each other permission to speak truth into each other's lives. Sometimes we would get angry and erupt, yell, even get in each other's faces. But we all knew we were committed to one another. Brotherly love gave us the freedom to be honest and direct when we needed to confront an issue. The result was that God used this group to bring about greater healing and maturity in each of us. God started working on one issue at a time, targeting things in our hearts that we needed to deal with. In essence, God was fathering us, and we were all moving toward greater wholeness. We were all growing in our identity as men, and we started to understand that we were sons of the King of kings. We were the King's men. We were priests, men of God; we were children of God Most High, dearly loved by our Father, and that made us special. It was the love and affirmation that I received through this men's group that gave me a revelation of the Father's heart toward me. This brought me to a whole new level of wholeness and functionality.

I later joined a home group and continued to attend the more personalized Small Ministry Team sessions offered by the church. I would receive prayer from two or three people at a time for one hour. These were concentrated sessions, and God started to go deeper. He started to excavate my very soul and lay a foundation in my life. In these sessions God continued healing the brokenness in my soul from rejection, abandonment, physical and emotional abuse, and performance orientation.

I was also getting free from a number of curses or labels that had been placed on me at a very young age. These were curses that the enemy had reinforced over the years through family, peers, teachers and coaches, and they were lies. Once these lies were broken off me, I was set free from many things that had bound me in the past. God began to speak truth, blessing and affirmation into my life through ministry team members, small groups, and my friends. Occasionally, God would have someone speak to me prophetically.

As God continued to heal me from the past, He started stripping away all the false personas I was hiding behind. Once God stripped away all of my props, defenses, and false identities, I felt completely naked. I distinctly remember after one particular session of healing, walking through the church sanctuary and feeling exceptionally vulnerable. God had been doing some major excavating. My false identity had been stripped away and I didn't know who I was. I hadn't yet been established in my spiritual identity, and I felt exposed, naked, and uncertain.

My temporary condition came home to roost one Sunday when I joined a men's breakfast after church at a nearby restaurant. I was sitting at the end of the table with about fourteen men roughly my age. The topics of conversation were mixed and varied. It was in the middle of all the conversation and sharing when a voice in my head screamed, *You have nothing to say! Nothing!* All of a sudden, I felt myself shrink in my chair, feeling like a little boy amidst all these men.

Later, I reflected on what had happened at the breakfast. It was obvious that part of me was still emotionally stunted, but by God's grace I began to grow and mature. Because I had acquired a false self, I had never developed emotionally beyond a certain point of trauma in my life. Consequently, I had been stuck in my boyhood. Eventually, I began to heal and grow, moving emotionally through adolescence into my mid-twenties. It was very awkward, going through adolescence in college when you are older than most of your peers. However, God continued to speak into my life, building me up, restoring all that had been stolen from me. I was so thankful for my God-given friends put in my life for such a time as this. God moved that year in miraculous and accelerated ways to heal and restore all of us, bringing about more wholeness in each of our lives.

I remember on one occasion being invited to the cafeteria by a friend. I thought he just wanted to talk since it was after the evening meal. When I arrived, all my friends were there with a birthday cake. With candles burning, they all said, "Happy birthday, David!" I never saw it coming. The demonstration of love completely caught me off guard, and as I looked around at all who had come to bless me, Tim Gray said, "We all love you Dave." That was it. I was completely undone, and before I could compose myself, I broke down sobbing at the table right in front of everybody. I was overwhelmed with emotion by this special demonstration of love. It was one of the most embarrassing, humbling, amazing, wonderful, and glorious experiences that I have ever had in my entire life! Moreover, God used it to bring about a profound healing in my heart.

It was moments like these that God used to begin rebuilding me. Little by little, I was becoming healthier and more whole. I was beginning to experience a confidence I had never known before as God was establishing and grounding me in my true identity. I truly understood, in the core of my being, that I was a man of God, dearly loved by the Savior.

I continued to grow in my identity in Christ. I also began to experience spiritual authority. I began to understand that Christ died and shed His blood to take away all the devil's rights to my life. Satan no longer had any access to attack me. His grounds had been removed. I was finally breaking free!

CHAPTER 22

Victorious!

IN THE "LORD OR THE Rings" trilogy, Gordo, Sam and a small band of friends unite to help each other complete a mission to destroy the Ring of Power. To do this, they cross miles of dangerous wilderness, fight against multitudes of evil Oarks, fight wild beasts, and sneak into the dark lord's stronghold. Then, and only then, can they cast the ring into the fires of Mount Doom where it will finally be destroyed, saving Middle Earth. It is a classic tale of good versus evil. In the end, good conquers evil and the heroes are victorious. This hard-fought war, the trials, testing and hardship that these characters endured, and the way they supported each other perfectly mirrored the challenges, struggles and emotional support that our band of brothers experienced in college.

By the middle of my sophomore year I was feeling like a new man. Little by little over the course of the semester, God was giving me more victory, and I was experiencing more freedom from pain in my life. This was true for my friends as well. We were beginning to understand who we were in Christ and our spiritual authority. Even better than that, we were beginning to exercise that authority. This didn't sit well with our spiritual adversaries who were becoming more displaced. Life on campus became very interesting, to say the least.

One night I was on security patrol. Twilight was approaching as two women walked up to me to report a strange man hanging around outside the women's dormitory. When I got there, I saw what looked like a homeless man. He was heavy-set, unshaven, and wore a dirty t-shirt and jeans. Moreover, he was walking around trying to look into the windows of the women's dorm rooms. He seemed to have no business there. I made my way over to the dormitory. I didn't know who this guy was, and I wanted to check him out first.

I approached him and said, "Hey man, what's going on?" The man just stared back at me with bulging eyes. His eyes were dilated and glassy, and I could see that he was obviously under the influence of alcohol or some kind of drug. As he continued to stare at me, he started to march in place without moving anywhere. As he did so, he began to sing the Marine Corps hymn.

"We will fight this country's battles, the United States Marines....Better watch it....Keep covering yourself with the blood." He made a hand motion across his forehead as he said it.

I had never even seen this man before in my life, so I knew at that moment that I was being mocked by a demon. This spirit obviously knew that I had served in the Marine Corps, and it also knew that I had been making it a practice to anoint my forehead with oil, praying the blood of Jesus over myself at night before going to bed.

Then I answered, "I know who you are, and you are going to lose."

The man's eyes glazed over; he staggered back. Then he said, "My name's Buddy, and Satan's in my skin!" He made another hand motion as he said it, as though injecting his arm with a needle. Then he turned, and ran as fast as he could down the street and disappeared around the corner. That was one of a few bizarre encounters I would have that year. I realized God's Spirit on me had frightened this demonized man away, and it gave me a sense of empowerment.

There was another occurrence one evening when I was off campus. Since I never had a lot of cash in college, I would often supplement my one meal plan in the cafeteria with Round Table Pizza breadsticks or Del Taco. On this occasion I was walking across a parking lot to my favorite restaurant, Del Taco, when I noticed three very loud, very drunk, and obnoxious men walking right toward me. They seemed rowdy and looked like they were going to be trouble, so I started praying against the spirits that I thought were influencing them. No sooner did I start praying than they suddenly changed direction and walked away from me.

On still another occasion, there was a late night when I was patrolling the campus. I was making my rounds and went into the men's dorm lobby. It was about midnight when I saw a tall, athletic-looking young man walking down the hallway, pounding very loudly on the walls as he went. I had seen him before and knew him to be living in the dorms but attending the college across the street. I had never met or talked to him before. I thought, *Wow! That's inconsiderate!*

I confronted him with, "Hey! Stop pounding on the walls! It's midnight! You're going to wake up everybody!" I yelled, waking up everybody in the process.

He just ignored me and continued down the hallway pounding. I followed and saw him disappear into his room toward the end of the hallway. I just thought, *I need to have a talk with this guy. This is just not ok.*

When I got to his room, I knocked a couple of times on his door. As soon as I finished knocking he came bursting out the door enraged. Pointing his finger in my face, he yelled at the top of his lungs, "You can't tell me what to do! I hate you! I'm sick of you, and I'm sick of your friends praying....!"

I instantly knew that a demon was manifesting in this guy, because I had never had any previous interaction with him. I also knew that the demon in this man was trying to draw me into a fight. It wanted to sabotage my future and God-ordained destiny. When the man yelled, he got right in my face. I backed up to give myself space. I then realized my back was against the wall. We were nose to nose. I could see the guy was amping up for a fight. His face was red. His adrenaline was increasing. His eyes were wide. His lips were pressed together. I knew that we were within seconds of going to blows....*At that moment, I saw a vision of myself in the principal's office, disappointment and regret on his face, as he tells me that I can no longer attend the college. The scene ends with the police hauling me away in handcuffs. Sorry, it's the end of the road for you, Mr. Jacques!* Not cool!

I then said as calmly as I could, "In Jesus' name, I bind the spirit of violence." The guy blinked a couple of times as though confused. Then I repeated myself again in a very low conversational tone, "I bind the spirit of violence in Jesus' name." He just stood there for a moment breathing hard. Then he yelled at the top of his lungs, "Fine!" Still breathing heavy, he walked back down the hallway and left the building. I had dodged another bullet, and I knew it. A physical altercation could have derailed my education and my future. I realized that I had just exercised my spiritual authority over a demon and that my faith had very practical use in the violent world I knew growing up.

I perceived that our spiritual adversary was hopping mad at all that God was doing with our group on campus. I was taking great pleasure in that. I thought, *after all the hell the devil put me through growing up, it feels good to finally get a little pay-back.* I was even more gleeful that I could apply my faith in such practical ways as to diffuse even physical altercations. I thought to myself, *All those years growing up as child, being picked on, abused by other kids, fighting on the playground, fighting all through school, and as a teenager, challenged time and time again by the next kid wanting to fight me...I realized beyond the shadow of a doubt, that it had all been demonic! All those years it had been demons marking me for destruction. It had been those unseen devils that had painted the target on my forehead. That's why trouble always found me, because it had been hunting me! I was the target of an unseen enemy that I knew nothing about. The answer had always been in my faith. The answer had always been Jesus! All those years it was the devil coming after me, but I knew nothing about the kingdom of darkness!*

Then I had another epiphany that night, and I was even more excited than before! *I realized that if I could discern and see what the enemy was doing, I could stop it, in the power and the authority of Jesus. I knew at that moment that I had total authority over my real enemy. Never again would I allow him to intimidate and manipulate me or my circumstances. I had total victory! I had total authority!* I went to the middle section of the dorms and sat in one of the booths so I could fully process what had just happened. I continued cogitating. *What other influence had the demonic played in my family's home life growing up?* My brain began to prickle with recognition as I began to remember all the nightmares as a child, the name-calling, the abuse by kids at school, the alcoholism, my parents' divorce and the destruction of my family. I knew that much of it had a demonic element to it, and that understanding it could have made a difference. My mind raced as I began to taste spiritual authority and victory over an unseen enemy that had haunted me my whole life. Suddenly, I was feeling empowered like never before!

I continued to process the implications of my new discovery. *God had certainly given me and my parents free will and the ability to choose right from wrong, but we never knew what we were actually dealing with. We never knew that demons were influencing us. We never understood fully what we were up against. Doors had been opened and access had been granted to an unseen saboteur, and we didn't know it! We were in a spiritual war the whole time, and we didn't know it! It was like shadow boxing in a dark room. We were fighting blind, and in our ignorance we played right into the devil's trap every time.* Only now I could see it clearly, and I knew that this revelation would change my life forever! I took a deep breath, realizing that my life would never be the same.

CHAPTER 23

Out of the Box

By my junior year of college I knew that my life would never be the same. This season of life was a major milestone for me and most of my friends. Tim, Arthur, Steve Burger and I continued meeting once a week, sharing our personal struggles and praying for each other through the ups and downs of college life and ministry. After experiencing the amazing power of God, we would never see church again in the same way. How could we ever go back to the way it was before? This learning curve had created a lot more questions than answers. God was completely out of the box and there was no putting Him back. *Everything used to be so neat and simple, so predictable and understandable. My systematic theology had God so neatly boxed. Now it seemed that He was breaking all the rules. Things would no longer be simple, predictable, and neatly packaged. God was blowing our comfort zone to smithereens. I realized there was no going back to the way it was. We couldn't go back even if we wanted to. Our lives would never be the same!*

It took us the first six months to realize that there was no set way to pray for people. I found this to be extremely exasperating. *Give me a method, a formula, a system! Give me a box, so I can put God back inside where He belongs!* But I continued to pray as God led me. One day on campus I ran into a student with an injured knee. He explained that he had injured it in a basketball game. I offered to pray for his injury, and he accepted. He sat down, and I knelt down to pray, laying my hands on his knee. As I began to pray, he told me that he was feeling a tingling sensation. The result was that he was healed and amazed all at the same time.

On another occasion I ran into someone with a broken arm in a splint. Knowing the words and the technique I had used before, I presumed that I now had the formula. This gave me confidence and enthusiasm as I launched into ministry, laying hands on the person and praying exactly the way I had done before. After all, it had worked before, right? However, to my bitter disappointment, nothing happened this time! Urrgh! One moment I would experience a major healing or miracle, and the next moment complete failure. God never contradicted Himself or His word, but He was constantly challenging my understanding.

For my friends and I, what was eventually burned into our minds was that God was not our tool. This was not "Star Wars," and this power was not "The Force" to wield at our will. We learned that we were *His* instruments, and that it was always about what He chose to do in any given situation. Steve Hampton had told us more than once, "Jesus only did that which He saw the Father doing." Yet, those words really didn't sink in at first. Many of these prayer situations required us to step out, risk, and take action. It was often hit or miss until we eventually learned to wait on God and listen to the Holy Spirit. And even then, we didn't always see what God was doing.

Hearing God's voice was another challenge. My assumptions had led me to believe that God's voice would be something grandiose and obvious. Over time I started to hear and discern the still, small voice of God. I learned that His voice often sounds like my own thoughts except that He often doesn't think like I do. I learned that God has absolutely no trouble speaking or communicating His will. He will even repeat himself, and even shout at times. However, if we persist in shutting Him out and refuse to listen, He will fall silent, something you never want Him to do.

Summer came around again. My security job was only part time, so I took a second job at the college in maintenance doing various odd jobs around campus. This usually involved moving large objects and emptying the trash cans. However, even these two jobs didn't provide enough income for me. I needed some full-time work, so I applied at the YMCA for the position of a summer day camp counselor. I was hired and worked there for a couple of summers. I drove a van, dropping off and picking up kids from a nearby park. The park was close to the facility and was a large grassy area with a sand pit, swings and monkey bars.

I would often go to the park on my lunch break to spend time with God. On one such occasion, I was walking around the park when I came across a heavy-set, older woman in a wheelchair. Her long, dark hair had gray streaks through it. When I asked how she was doing, she explained that she was suffering from lupus, and that her condition was so advanced that it had confined her to a wheelchair. Moreover, she said that the most routine, everyday tasks would overwhelm and exhaust her.

As I spoke with her further, I remembered hearing a pastor give a testimony that lupus was also known as wolf's disease, and that God had told him to command the wolf spirit to leave. A successful healing followed after the pastor's prayer. I then asked her if I could pray for her. She said that she wouldn't mind at all. So with her permission, I laid my hands on her shoulders and started to pray. As I did, God reminded me of that pastor's testimony. He had said something like, "You filthy, stinking dog, leave her!" He later testified to literally seeing a spirit slink away like a dog.

I was feeling a lot of faith and decided to try this. So as I started praying, I asked God to release His healing touch. Immediately power began surging through my hand. With the power came an increase in my faith, so I asked for more power. The surges increased. The woman seemed entranced under the power. Then I spoke to the spirit of lupus and said, "You filthy, stinking dog, leave her in Jesus' name." I then repeated the same prayer. I continued praying until I sensed that it was over. She thanked me for the prayer, and I left.

I was back at the park a week later. That day I saw the same lady I prayed for standing in her front yard across the street watering her lawn. When she saw me, she smiled and gave an exuberant wave. I waved back, happy to see her out of the wheelchair and feeling better. I thought to myself, *God is awesome!*

The following week I was working on another warm summer day at the Y. At the end of the day the parents were coming to pick up their kids. I always got along with the kids, and most of the parents were nice people. However, one woman started to look at me in a weird way. She was blond and had a rough complexion. She looked to be in her mid-thirties, and she began to fixate on me. I could never figure out why. Well, as the parents were signing out their kids, I was bringing her child up front to get signed out.

Then out of the blue, she walked up to me and, in a hushed tone, said, "I don't want you touching my boy, and I don't want you near him." I was caught completely off guard by her statement and attitude. I just stood there speechless as she led her little boy away by the hand, breaking eye contact with me only after she had turned around. Her words were cutting. My stomach sank. I felt discouraged, angry and misunderstood. As discouragement set in, I contemplated how she must have perceived me. I thought about what she might be telling other parents. My imagination ran wild with all the possible scenarios that could be brewing behind the scenes just out of that single comment. What if she files a complaint? What if she accuses me of molesting her kid? In this day, you are considered guilty until proven innocent just for the accusation! I could lose my job or worse!

Two weeks later, I was at the end of a day at the park with all the kids from the Y and two other counselors. The other counselors were loading the kids onto the vans. I was helping to round up the stragglers when this accusing mother accosted me again. She had come to pick up her child early. This time she narrowed her eyes and asked in an accusing tone, "Why do you want to work with children so badly?" (Accusing tone, implying there must be more to it). She didn't wait for an answer. Apparently, her mind was already made up. She just turned and walked away from me, retrieving her child as she left.

At that point I thought, *I need to tell someone about this, report it to my supervisor.* That day came and went, and I didn't get around to saying anything until Wednesday of the following week. When I described the situation to Mary, the program director, she was just picking up a toddler. When she realized who I was talking about, she raised her eyebrows and said, "You know she passed away."

"What?...Who passed away?" It didn't quite register with me.

"That boy's mom, this weekend, they found her in her apartment. They say she had a heart attack." She spoke while bouncing the child on her hip. "Her boy is no longer with us. He's gone to live with his grandmother in Texas."

I just stood there speechless. I spent the rest of that day contemplating what had happened. *Did God come to my defense by taking this woman's life? Would God actually do something like that? Was that even possible? After all, who am I that God would defend me in such a way?* I would never know for sure. I took no pleasure in her death, and it wasn't something that I would've wished on anyone, even my worst enemy. In my mind God was completely out of the box. At the end of the day, I was left feeling humbled and awestruck.

CHAPTER 24

Divine Director

IT SEEMED OUR SMALL BAND of believers was in the very center of God's hands, and that he was orchestrating all our circumstances. He was working, bringing everything together. Summer came and went. I was now in the middle of my fourth year of college. My desk was lost under stacks of books and homework. One day when winter mid-terms were approaching, I had two major term-papers due. I was buried in studies when my friend J-Michael came to visit. He was small in stature with dark, wavy, shoulder length hair. However, what J-Michael lacked in height, he more than made up for in boldness of faith. I had been cracking the books for a good three hours when He asked if I wanted to go across the street to Cal State Fullerton, walk around, and share our faith with some of the students over there. My brain was feelin' kind of fried, so I thought it would be a welcome break.

When we got to the neighboring college, we couldn't help but notice a very loud punk band performing an outdoor concert in the middle of campus. As the band played on, we began to discern a darkness around the college. For one thing, the music was dark and loud, and the lyrics were filled with obscenities. As expletives continued to pour forth from the band, we knew that this would hinder our efforts, making it impossible to reach people.

Since it was an outdoor concert, J-Michael suggested, "Hey... why don't we just call down rain to stop the concert? Then we can witness to people." He was the type of guy who would believe God for anything, and his faith stretched and challenged me often. I looked up and noticed that it was overcast, so I actually believed there was a chance that God might do this. We started praying, agreeing together and asking God to send rain. We then began calling down rain. After about five minutes, which seemed like a very long time, we both felt a sprinkle. We went ballistic! Our faith increased as we got louder and bolder in shouting down the rain! The rain then started to come in steady; we were beside ourselves. We started to shout, "More, Lord! More, Lord! As we shouted, the rain began to come down heavy. The more we asked for, the heavier the rain came!

To our amazement, the band continued to play. They seemed unfazed and unconcerned about their electrical equipment. Their faces looked pensive, determined. The battle was on! We asked God for more rain, and the rain got even heavier than before. The rain continued to pummel the band. Eventually they just had to stop. The rain was just too heavy as the full-blown monsoon continued. When the band finally stopped, J-Michael and I walked the hallways talking to students about Jesus. We even had the opportunity to pray for some. It was an amazing break from the books, and afterward I went back to my studies feeling completely amped on what God had done.

Going into our last year of college, the spiritual awakening of our little campus group had sparked our zeal to see the rest of our evangelical brothers and sisters come into all the fullness of God. We had a vision to see our whole college experiencing a spiritual renewal. I think our zeal and our immaturity may have been interpreted by others as pride, condescension or insensitivity. In truth, it was just unbridled passion. We had been awakened to the tangible reality of God's power, of angels, of demons, and the miracle realm. This was all new to us and having a direct impact on our day-to-day existence. Virtually overnight, the Bible had gone from being a history book to a written example of what we were experiencing first hand on a daily basis. Yet as we looked around, we were seeing a student body living ho-hum, spiritual lives. For them it was business-as-usual, and we found it disconcerting.

Consequently, we felt a need to do something about it. Since we had developed the habit of anointing others with oil for healing and deliverance (James 5), we all thought that our college could be awakened by anointing *it* with oil as well. We discussed this at length and came up with a plan to anoint the whole college. We decided who would get the oil, who would get the bucket, and who would bring the hand towels.

Our goal was to anoint the school with oil and pray over it for a spiritual awakening into the miracle realm of signs and wonders. We believed spiritual blinders would then be removed from the faculty and the student body, opening their eyes to the spiritual realm. This would result in a greater understanding, discernment, and perception. There would be a widespread visitation of the manifest presence of God's Spirit on campus accompanied by miracles, signs and wonders. We would see a visible increased zeal and passion for worship and the things of the Spirit. Then we would all be embraced and understood instead of being perceived as the campus kooks.

Now, as kooky as that may sound, it really made sense to us. Our band of brothers chose a night in the middle of the week when we knew most of the students would turn in early. We waited until after midnight, and we all dressed in dark clothing. We must have looked like wannabe Ninjas. One of us brought a bucket and we filled it with some vegetable oil, and we all brought hand towels. Then we gathered around the bucket, and prayed a blessing to anoint the oil. We started at the far side of the college. Then dipping our hand towels in the oil, we ran around anointing all the columns of the college buildings. The columns were large, square, concrete structures painted white. We made sure that we anointed all four sides of each column in the sign of the cross. By the time we finished, every column and lamp post in the college had a cross on it painted in oil. There were a lot of columns, and we made sure that we did both floors. The oil was a clear liquid, so we figured it would just wash off, or at least not show.

We were *wrong!* The next day, crosses shown on each of the columns throughout the college as the oil was absorbed into the porous, flat, white paint leaving a clear, glossy, indelible impression of a cross. The faculty's usual suspects were not difficult to figure out. When we realized that the oil was showing up like a sore thumb and stained indelibly, that's when the nail biting started. Obviously, the mature thing would have been to admit our crime, confess our sin, and ask for mercy, if not forgiveness, right? Instead, we agreed to remain silent on the matter.

A day later, the oldest and most mature member of our party made a unilateral decision to tell the faculty! After he told the faculty what we'd done, he came to us and told us that the jig was up, and that he had confessed. We were incredulous but repentant, and we forgave our brother for ratting us out! When we were called into the principal's office, I was thinking, *This is it. We're busted!* As we waited to be seen, I kept wondering about the outcome. I figured we had essentially vandalized and graffitied the whole school. I also figured that the cost of paint it would take to cover everything we had marked could be substantial. Regardless, we would need to make things right. We could offer to buy the paint ourselves, and we could do the labor ourselves. Problem solved!

We soon discovered we were not facing Principal Montgomery but Professor Allen Ferrell again, a much better deal. Nonetheless, we were nervous and on edge as we took our seats. Mr. Ferrell sat there quietly, waiting on the edge of his desk with one foot on the floor and the other swinging slightly.

Although Mr. Ferrell was not an intimidating man, we all felt like children in trouble with their parents.

He finally spoke, "Hi guys. I guess you all know why you are here today." He said it as he scanned us back and forth with his eyes. "David," I sat up at attention. "I was told that you were the ring leader for this little...venture. Would you like to explain what this is all about?"

I started right in. "First, we all planned this together, Mr. Ferrell."

He cocked his head as though to hear me better. "And?"

"We thought it would be a good idea to anoint the college with oil and pray over it to stop any demonic interference against the school," I said matter-of-factly. "We didn't know the oil would stain the columns. We can buy paint and paint the columns if you'd like, no problem." The other two agreed, nodding their heads in unison.

Mr. Ferrell sat there looking down and trying to hold back a smile. Then he looked up. "That will not be necessary; the school was already planning to repaint the college, so you are off the hook this time. You just moved up the school's project date, that's all."

Breathing out relief, we all chimed in: "Oh, that's great! Really! Fantastic! We really appreciate your understanding!"

Then he said something unexpected, "Some of us are rooting for you guys, but *please*, use discretion. Try to be aware of where other people are in their faith." We continued talking for a while, and left shaking hands and feeling like a major weight had been lifted from our shoulders. We were exuberant, excited, and anticipating the future. We all had the conviction that God's hand was on our lives, and that He was divinely directing us.

That college year went by quickly. Although I had taken a second part-time job doing maintenance to help with expenses, the responsibilities were fairly light. Mostly, I just made sure that the trash cans around campus were emptied once a day. With one other guy, I would go around replacing the plastic bags, tying off the full bags and dumping them in a nearby trash bin. At night I would continue to function as security, locking down the classrooms and making my usual patrol around campus.

One day I was emptying trash cans and changing out the liners. It was getting toward the end of the spring semester and was a very hot and muggy day in May. I was underneath the stairwell to the library trying to stay cool. I had worn a dirty t-shirt and blue jeans for emptying trash cans. By the time I finished, I was filthy, and I'm sure that I didn't smell too good when Tamba rounded the corner. She was alone, and before I could think to be embarrassed, she was standing right there in front of me. Even as she stood before me, I noticed an absence of fear. It was almost strange. A deep sense of peace rested within my soul. I felt sound. There was a new strength and stability in my spirit.

My instant response was to embrace her, and as I did she melted into my arms. I said, "I love you so much."

She answered back in a voice muffled against my shoulder, "I love you, too." We held each other for a wonderful moment, and she stepped back smiling.

"Congratulations!" She said. "You made it! You'll be graduating." I looked into those light green eyes and felt like she was gazing into my very soul.

I said "Thanks. You did too."

Finally realizing what I must look like, I grew self-conscious. We struggled with some small talk for a while. Then she said, "Good-bye, David."

"Good-bye, Tamba."

As she walked away, I noticed that I was feeling joy, and a lot more wholeness. I think that she could see it too. God had done a miracle in my life. I reflected for a while about all that God had done. We both knew things would never be the same between us, but for the first time in my life, I was okay with that. I was *really* okay, and it felt good. I knew God was acting as the Divine Director of our lives, and I thanked Him for bringing everything full-circle.

CHAPTER 25

Graduation Day

EVERYTHING WAS ABUZZ ON GRADUATION day. Students donned their caps and gowns as relatives hovered around the dorm rooms. I was dressed and ready to meet my dad in front of the dorm. Dad arrived to pick me up and drive me. Mom planned to meet us there at the ceremony. When we got there, the parking lot was already packed. I felt a nervous excitement and anticipation, understanding this to be an important rite of passage for me.

It turned out that the only facility large enough and close enough to the college for our graduating class was Anaheim Vineyard Christian Fellowship. *Talk about all things coming together! The school, the church, and the friends who all had shaped the course of my life, gathered all in one place at one time. This must be heaven! What are the odds?* Dad and I entered the church, looking around the lobby for any familiar faces. Then we spotted Mom. She approached with her face beaming.

"I'm so proud of you! She said, tearing up. I love you!" Then she gave me a tight squeeze around the neck and a kiss on the cheek.

"I love you too, Mom."

She gave me that proud, parent look.

Preoccupied, I said, "Aaah...I really need to get ready now. I'll talk to you both later, okay?"

"Ok, see you soon," Mom said.

The music started, and I ran to where I needed to be and stood with the other graduates. The ceremony ran its course like a well-oiled machine. We all filed in and took our seats as Pomp and Circumstance played in the background. Principal Montgomery called the name of each student and smiled wide, congratulating and shaking each student's hand as he presented their well-earned diploma. The faculty sat in rows on stage in their gowns and honor garb. They also shook hands, greeting each of the graduates filing past. In the end, everyone threw their caps in the air like one big Frisbee toss. Before I knew it, it was over.

I went straight to the lobby to have one last rally with my friends and to say goodbye. Instead, I found Tamba's mother Cheryl who greeted me with a tight squeeze. With an enthusiastic smile and a playful shake of my shoulders, she said, "You made it! Congratulations!" I saw forgiveness in her eyes. Right then the guys found me and wanted to get a picture together. Cheryl offered to take the picture. We stood together, linked arms, and posed like embattled and triumphant soldiers at the end of a hard-fought war.

Although I had gained a lot more confidence, my emotions were mixed. Extreme joy and sadness began to vie for position in my heart. This was by far one of the greatest moments in my life. Not only was I graduating from college, but I was also embarking on a whole new chapter of my life, this time as a whole new person. I would be experiencing life from a whole new, enhanced perspective, now as a healthier, more secure man. I was also excited that my band of brothers had similar bright futures ahead of them.

We all knew that God had brought us to a new horizon in our lives, and that He alone would lead us into the future. We kept trying to postpone the inevitable good-byes as we continued to linger after graduation. Finally, our talk grew thin. With backslaps and hugs we all said our farewell to one another and went our separate ways. It was the end of a significant season in my life.

CHAPTER 26

Promised Land

FAST FORWARD...THOUGH I WAS A considerably healthier man after college, I didn't seriously date anyone for quite some time. I was determined to wait on God for the right woman. I moved to Ventura County, California, where I worked as a youth pastor and in other ministries. Ventura is a small beach community nestled on a beautiful coastline. With its miles of beaches, numerous bike paths, and nearby mountains, it became a recreational paradise for me. Having come from a largely metropolitan area, Ventura's small town ambiance seemed to be the best of both worlds.

I was also involved in a large ministry consisting of 200 singles. It was there that I met a guy named Roland who organized group hikes which were lots of fun and brought local Christian singles together. I enjoyed the activity, hiked as often as I could, and made many friends. Eventually Roland met a young woman and began dating. Their eventual marriage took them out of the singles ministry virtually overnight.

Roland's absence left a gap in the leadership. I volunteered to pick up the baton to keep the hikes going. Between eight and twelve people regularly showed up for hikes. Leading these hikes was very satisfying for me, and I enjoyed the community it created.

As the holidays approached, one of the larger churches in our area planned a singles' dinner which I decided to attend. On this Saturday evening, I walked into a large event room. The room was set with round tables and white tablecloths with flower vases as centerpieces. As I entered, there were a couple of women handing out the evening itinerary. One was hard to overlook. She was very striking, and I remember thinking, *Now that's my type of girl right there! I've never seen her before. Wow, she's a knock-out!* She looked like the quintessential California Girl. Her green eyes and all-American features got my attention right away. As she stood there passing out the event schedule, I thought, *I've got to meet this girl!*

When I approached her, she greeted me and gave me an itinerary. I said "Hi, my name's David!"

"I'm Lori!" she said with this dazzling smile.

It was starting to get noisy in the room, so I leaned in and asked, "Do you hike, Lori?"

"Yes, I do." She said.

At that moment, I had a brain freeze. My mind went blank. All of a sudden, I was completely out of material, so I said, "Nice meeting you, Lori." With that, I walked away. I spent the next week kicking myself. *The girl of my dreams, and I just walk away! Why didn't I talk to her? Why didn't I get her contact information?* I went on and on in my head like this, kicking myself for quite a while.

A week later when New Year's Eve rolled around, a very large mega-church was hosting a singles' New Year's Eve dinner/dance out of town. I decided to go since I knew a lot of the people who would be there. When I arrived I bought my ticket at the door and made my way toward the tables in a very large, ballroom sized place. The room was decorated with streamers and shiny foiled stars hanging from the ceiling. There was a DJ, and the attire ranged from formal to semi-formal. Large round tables dotted the room donned in white tablecloths, confetti, and party favors. I was looking for familiar faces when my eyes flashed across her form. I had to consciously keep myself calm. *There she is again, that girl I met at the Christmas dinner!* She was standing over near the wall talking to a couple of guys. *Her name...Lori is her name!*

I went over and stood near her group until we made eye contact. Then I said hello and walked over to talk to her. I noticed that she had pretty eyes and long lashes. Her face was glowing with radiance, and the skin on her arms looked like honey. I was entranced. Everybody else seemed to fade into the background. As far as I was concerned, she was the only one in the room.

I said, "Hey, you said that you like to hike, right?"

"Uh huh," she said nodding.

"Well, a group of us are going to hike next Saturday. You're welcome to join us if you'd like!"

"Ok, that'd be great!" she said with that gorgeous smile.

"Great! If I can get your contact information, I'll see to it that you get all the details," I said with confidence brimming.

She fished out a pen from her purse and wrote her name, number, and email address in perfect cursive writing. Then she handed her information to me. I told her that I would be right back. Not wanting to take the chance of losing her information, I bounded back to my car, jumping in exultation over the note in hand. I stashed the prized info in my car's center console. Then I raced back to the party. When I got back to the door, I stopped, calmed myself down, and walked casually back. I found Lori sitting with an older gentleman. He looked to be about ten years her senior. I had seen her with him earlier. Then it occurred to me that he might be her date for the evening.

I sat down beside her opposite him. He was about six feet tall and had dark hair starting to gray on the sides. As we talked, I discreetly asked Lori if they were dating, and she told me they had just come as friends. I thought to myself. *There's no way that's what he was thinking. He had to have been hoping for something more than friendship.*

One conversation led to the next; Lori and I talked all night. I learned that she was from Minnesota and had been divorced for a number of years. She had just recently decided to start going out again. She told me that she had two children, twins who were seven, a boy and a girl, and that she had just moved out to California for a fresh start. As I shared some of my story, she shared that she had come from a family with a missionary background and had also graduated from a Christian college. As we continued sharing, *I kept listening to my own spirit, trying to detect any sense of fear or anxiety within myself. Was I truly whole? Was I really ready for a relationship?* We continued to talk, and we danced a little later to some retro big band and Sinatra tunes. We danced a slow dance, and she felt good in my arms.

I left that evening feeling higher than a kite. There was something about this woman, something I had never experienced before. There was a peace and wholesomeness to her character, and I intuitively knew that she was a woman of substance. It turned out to be a wonderful night.

Our first date was a group hike through Wildwood Park. The park with its trees, rolling hills, waterfalls and stream crossings, possessed a certain charm. We hiked up about five-hundred feet to a place called Lizard Rock. I was pleasantly surprised that Lori was more than able to keep up. I thought hiking would be a good first date because of the nature of the activity. I figured it would help me sense her predisposition for the outdoors. I was pleasantly surprised to learn that she genuinely enjoyed the activity; moreover, she was in great shape.

This first hike was a short, easy, three miler. I thought it would allow us to talk and get to know each other at our leisure. That didn't happen. A very good friend of mine, Paul, kept her engaged in conversation throughout the hike! I continued to socialize with the other singles, but in the back of my mind I was asking myself some serious questions. *Was I truly healed? Was I now whole and healthy enough for a relationship? Would I be able to sustain the relationship long term, or would I unravel again? Would fear once again undermine my confidence and sabotage my dating relationship?* These thoughts ran through the back of my mind as I was getting to know Lori. It wasn't that I didn't feel confident. I did. *But would my confidence suddenly evaporate? Would it take a vacation? Would another relationship blow up in my face?*

Later, I scheduled some hikes that were considerably more challenging. The next hike was up Boney Mountain, a high, steep mountain trail in Thousand Oaks. The word was that the mountain had been created by a lava flow. It was known to be a very challenging climb with almost three thousand foot gain in elevation in just five miles. I picked Lori up for the hike, and we met the others at the trailhead. It was a sunny, clear day, and the hike started off fairly casual as people talked and socialized. People conversed while enjoying the increasingly panoramic views. When we took the Danielson Trail the socializing waned because the trail became very narrow.

We stopped momentarily at the Danielson monument which was a low, square, brick wall often used for a rest stop, and then we began to move toward the top. After the Danielson Monument the mountain trail became steeper and more treacherous. Conversation grew thin. We entered a heavily wooded Manzanita forest. The mountain grew even steeper and the narrow path created almost a tunnel effect. The ground was mostly loose rock and gravel. Past rainstorms had eroded much of the trail creating deep, wide trenches that split the trail in half. This required us to hike on one side of the split or the other. In addition, the heat of the day had increased. We took breaks when necessary and drank lots of water. As we approached the top of the mountain, the grade began to develop into a steady, radical rise to the top. I noticed that Lori had picked up her pace. She had very strong, tan, athletic legs that were more than a match for the mountain. Not wanting her to get to the summit before I did, *I can't be outdone by my date*, I began to race up the rocks getting to the top just before she did, barely. When we got to the summit we both stopped and caught our breath while waiting for the rest of the group. Right then and there I knew this was the girl for me! When the rest of the group caught up, we all had lunch at the top. There was a crisp, ocean breeze coming over the mountain. It was sunny and the sky was a cloudless blue which seemed to sharpen my focus on this amazing woman.

Lori and I talked and got to know each other better over the course of the next few weeks, playing "twenty questions" by email. I learned about Lori's two children. I also learned that she was wonderful in every way. The more time we spent together, the more peace I felt. Soon we were hiking together on a regular basis. I learned that she was sound, practical, grounded, and fun-loving. These qualities only served to secure my interest. Eventually, we were dating and seeing each other continually as well as attending church together. After a year of dating, I felt that I was finally ready and mature enough for marriage. I asked her to marry me.

We decided to get married on New Year's Day at Ventura Vineyard Church. With rock rhythm worship music playing in the background, we mingled with friends and family and sought out those we hadn't seen for a while to catch up on old times. Each of us met family, hugged friends, and kissed our moms and dads. Before we knew it, vows had been given, pictures taken, hands shaken, and the wedding cake cut. Not only was the wedding cake cut, but also the ties to my dark past that had prevented me from having a healthy relationship. Praise God!

Our honeymoon plan was to drive north up the California coast while Lori's two kids stayed with relatives. I had arranged for our first night to be spent in a treehouse cottage in Solvang. Later we visited Big Sur, Cambria, Morro Bay, and the Monterey Aquarium. It was an incredible week! I recognized right away that God had brought me to a new place of blessing, my promised land. I knew that time would test the substance of our marriage, but Lori had already proven to be a woman of integrity. I figured that my ability to sustain a long term relationship would be tested and proven within three years.

The next thing I knew, we were back home. We were now planning and leading hikes together as a church activity, but now for both marrieds and singles. We had hiked a number of the local mountains in our area, places like Nordhoff Peak, Topa Topa, Half Dome and San Gorgonio. I developed a passion for the mountains. It seemed being out in the wilderness always helped me to connect with God. Now I had a wife equally passionate about the outdoors, and I couldn't be happier.

I was amazed at what God had done in my life taking me from the deepest, darkest emotional valley to the mountaintop. God had blessed me with a woman who genuinely loved the things that I loved. Every hike and every mountain was a new challenge for us, and we looked forward to taking them on together. Life had become a whole new adventure, and God was about to take us to our highest mountaintop...literally!

CHAPTER 27

The Mountaintop

FAST FORWARD ... THREE YEARS later Lori and I are still married! Hallelujah! Even after three years we are still getting to know each other. We had set a goal to summit Mount Whitney in one day, so we began to prepare for the climb. What I didn't realize was that this climb would become a spiritual metaphor for all that God had done in my life. Whitney was the mother of all hikes. The mountain represented, for me, the seemingly insurmountable bondage, fear, and brokenness in my life. It was the monster that threatened to devour me. Reaching the summit would be analogous to arriving at a place of freedom and victory.

We discovered that Mt. Whitney was 14,497 feet in elevation and was the highest mountain in the lower forty-eight states. We learned that it would be a twenty-two mile round trip. We also knew that we would need to train for this marathon of all day-hikes. It would be a challenge every bit as daunting as my own journey toward healing. I would need to train and prepare for this hike with the same commitment I had in getting spiritually healthy. Lori was also committed and enthusiastic but nervous. She had never liked heights.

Not long after we were married I learned about Lori's fear of heights when we climbed the backside of Half Dome in Yosemite. It was somewhat crowded that day. We had been climbing the cables together when I decided to go around the more traveled inside center and ascend the cables from the outside to make better time. Before I went, I turned and asked Lori if she would be all right. Not wanting to hold me back, she said yes. I took off toward the top, pulling myself up by the cables as I went. When

I got to the top I joined another friend who was very fast and quite athletic. We both sat and waited for Lori. After about five minutes I became concerned, knowing that she should have been to the top by now. I got up and walked over to the shoulder of the mountain and looked over the edge. I looked down to see Lori frozen in place on the cable. When I got down to her she was in tears. I coaxed her up until we both arrived at the top. I held her in my arms until she calmed down from her fear of the dizzying height. I had not understood her fear until then. I had seen her on many occasions power through precarious trails in spite of her aversion to heights. I figured going down Half Dome would be even more difficult for Lori since we would be looking down from an elevation of 8,839 feet. Nevertheless, she made it down, and continued to train time and again, defying her fear.

Our major concern was AMS (acute mountain sickness). AMS was something I had experienced first-hand as we were attempting to summit San Gorgonio in the San Bernardino Mountain range. I had started the hike with very little sleep after a demanding week. The peak was 11,503 feet. Though we made it to the summit, it came with a price. After hitting the 9,000 foot mark, I started feeling a mild headache. I thought nothing of it at the time. It was odd because I'm usually not affected by elevation. By the time we passed 10,000 feet, my head just didn't feel right, like I was in a dull fog. By the time I realized that I should be descending, we were already at the summit. The summit marker imbedded into the rock read: "San Gorgonio Wilderness, Elevation: 11, 503 feet." I touched the trail marker to make it official that I had reached the top, but I was not having fun. My head ached. As we started down, I began to get dizzy and disoriented almost losing the trail at one point. We moved quickly down the mountain. Once I hit the 9,000 ft. mark, I completely recovered and was once again in my right mind. It was, however, a lesson I would never forget. I learned that elevation puts stress on your body through pressure changes that can literally become debilitating. I thought how, in a similar way, the pressures of life can be debilitating as well. A break-up, divorce, loss of a job, financial setback, bankruptcy, or a sudden death in the family, can leave us overwhelmed and even incapacitated. At this point in my life, I was relieved to be without that kind of stress. The stress of climbing a mountain can be more easily overcome.

Finally, we were ready for our next hiking challenge, Mount Whitney. We left town on a Thursday and drove up Highway 395 through the desert to Lone Pine. It was a long drive with miles of flat desert and triple-digit temperatures. I drove a car that I had questionable confidence in. The engine was reliable enough, but in the desert it wasn't uncommon to see drivers stopping because of vehicles overheating. I really didn't want to be one of them. On this desert journey I stared out, panning the road and the hot dry landscape, thinking about how my life had been like one dry, emotionally barren desert before coming to Christ. I thought, *it had taken an emotional breakdown before I recognized my need to take the journey toward healing and recovery.* We drove on as miles of dry, hot landscape dotted with Joshua trees and cactus rolled by.

We headed toward Lone Pine, California, a small western town. The heat was fierce outside when we got there. We stopped at a local diner for a meal before driving up to the Whitney Portal where we spent the first night acclimating.

Whitney Portal is where the trailhead is located. We got there and looked up at Mt. Whitney, its peaks like the large, jagged teeth of a monster waiting to gobble us up. It was intimidating. We then turned to look for our reserved campsite. We knew from experience that the campsite was a major thoroughfare for black bears. On a previous expedition we had had several bears wandering in and out of our campsite at night. Lori informed me later that she had been on high alert early that morning. She was hearing heavy, growly breathing outside our tent at 4:00am. I found out that Lori had sat up awake all night holding up my Ka-bar with both hands. She said that she tried to shake me awake, but I was sleeping too soundly. However, I awoke when the early morning silence was broken by a camper yelling at a bear.

This particular camper had decided to sleep out under the stars. A hot breath in his face woke him up to behold a black bear staring down at him. With a rush of adrenaline and excitement, he immediately sat up.

"Yaw! Yaw! Get out of here!," the camper shouted. The bear quickly backed away staring at him for a moment, and then walked off.

On that occasion, the bears were all gone by daybreak. However, Lori never let me forget that I slept while her very *life* was in danger! I couldn't help but compare these large growling beasts that emerge at night to the spiritual beasts (demons) that had tormented me at night in the past.

After setting up camp, we had been careful to lock up food in the bear box provided in each campsite. I was told that bears can smell food miles away tracking the scent and eventually finding the source of that smell. *It's the same spiritually,* I thought. *Demonic spirits are attracted to garbage in our lives. Unforgiveness, bitterness, lust, jealousy, slander, rebellion, gossip, and witchcraft draw dark spirits that desire to attach themselves to a person to gain power and influence over them.* As with the bears, constant vigilance is needed.

We spent most of that first day setting up camp, resting, and acclimating to the 9,000 foot elevation. We had been taking an herbal supplement to prevent acute mountain sickness. With all our planning we didn't want our trip to be cut short because of some symptom of AMS. Another concern was that a thunderstorm broke at about one o'clock in the afternoon.

As we began talking to other hikers we learned that at roughly the same time every day, there was an electrical storm on the mountain. Lori was understandably concerned, being the more sensible of the two of us. After some discussion, we figured that if we left at ten o'clock at night we could reach the summit before twelve noon, eat our lunch, and begin our descent before the afternoon storm.

The following day we continued acclimating. Even though we were supposed to be resting, we were both experiencing a nervous energy, something between excitement and an awesome respect for the mountain. We had heard stories of hikers losing their lives on the mountain. We both knew that the hike would have a strong mental component to it. It would be similar to my journey toward healing in that it required a resolute commitment to keep moving forward and never quitting.

That night we tried to force ourselves to sleep but could only rest due to nervous excitement. We both knew that this mountain would be daunting and potentially dangerous. It would challenge us both physically and mentally. Before long it was nearing ten o'clock, and we were gearing up in the night chill. After praying together for safety, we started hiking. The night was quiet and pitch black. Similar to my sojourn through healing and recovery, I would be starting this journey in darkness. I thought about how I began my recovery in the darkness of my understanding with no discernment of the spirit realm. That night on the mountain nothing was visible except our breath as it fogged the night air in the beam of our headlamps. Without our headlamps illuminating the trail in front of us, we would have been stumbling around in the dark. In that same moment I realized that without the illumination of God's word, I would still be stumbling through life in spiritual darkness. It was only when God intervened in my life that I began to see the path clearly. *"Thy word is a lamp unto my feet and a light unto my path."* Psalm 119:105 KJV

Before attempting to climb Mt. Whitney, we had planned and prepared ourselves. I knew this hike would be a long haul; however, I was committed and invested in the journey. Had I not committed myself, I would have never made it. Likewise, I had to be just as committed to my journey through recovery or I would never have made it.

We started our 10.7 mile ascent up the mountain. The first mile was quiet and dark with nothing but our headlamps illuminating the trail in front of us. The first mile is always significant. That's when your blood is getting pumped into your muscles, and your muscles are getting oxygen. It's the warming-up phase when you are working out any aches and pains. The most dangerous periods in any major hike are at the beginning and the end. The beginning is dangerous because your muscles are still cold. You're not stretched out yet, so pulling or straining a muscle is much easier to do. The end of a hike is dangerous because you're tired and fatigued and much more inclined to make careless mistakes or sprain an ankle. That first mile we were feeling good. We passed the Mountaineer's Route and started up the mountain. After hiking steady for an hour, we looked back down the mountain to see several teams of hikers in the cold night, only visible by their headlamps snaking their way up the mountain, like luminescent worms in the dark.

When we neared Lone Pine Lake, we came to a stream crossing. Our headlamps illuminated stepping stones for a rock bridge submerged in the shallows. It was dark, and the water was freezing cold. I used my hiking poles to balance across the stream quickly. Lori began taking off her boots and socks.

"What are you doing Lori?"
"Taking off my socks."
"I know that. Why?"
"I don't want to hike in wet socks."

"You know that water is going to be freezing cold, don't you?"

"I'm from Minnesota. I'm familiar with cold water. Besides, they'll warm up. My dad didn't raise no wimps."

I just rolled my eyes, "Ooo-k."

Lori proceeded across the stream without a word, to my utter astonishment. When she got to the other side, she dried her feet with a small towel, and put her socks and boots back on. When she was ready, we continued up to Lone Pine Lake and on to Big Horn. We passed Mirror Lake and Trail Side Meadows. We were regretting missing these beautiful places in the dark. I thought about how we often miss out on the beauty in life because we choose to walk in spiritual darkness. However, spiritual darkness is far worse than the darkness we were experiencing on the trail that night.

A big concern was running into bears in the dark, perhaps surprising a mother with cubs. That would be bad. I figured that our trail was well traveled and that bears would mostly stay clear of it. At the six mile mark we came to Trail Camp. This area was right at the foot of a very steep ascent called the Ninety-Seven Switchbacks which would take us up to Trail Crest. For safety, we didn't want to start up the switchbacks in the dark. Our headlamps wouldn't give us enough illumination. Only the sun would provide enough light to negotiate the trail. Spiritually, only the Son of God provided enough light to restore me to wholeness. I needed Jesus, the Son of God Himself, to infuse His truth into my very soul. The Great Physician healed me and set me free, making me into a functional and healthy human being capable of climbing this mountain with the woman I love.

It was now about four in the morning, so we decided to rest for a couple of hours and wait for daybreak before starting up the switchbacks. It was still very cold. We threw a small tarp over ourselves and used our backpacks as pillows. We slept back-to-back for warmth. Soon, we began to hear scratching and rustling sounds in our backpacks. The field mice were relentless and not shy in the least. This was distracting, because I didn't want them to chew through our backpacks and destroy our gear. Lori kept feeling mice crawling over her. We didn't really sleep, but got some well-needed rest.

At daybreak, we started up the Ninety-Seven Switchbacks. This was Lori's least favorite part of the expedition. It was high and steep with rapid elevation gain. As we were approaching the last of the switchbacks, we came to a place where the winter snow and ice had worn away the trail. The erosion had turned a very narrow trail into nothing more than a soft shoulder, barely discernible, with at least a two-thousand foot drop off the edge. This was one of the obstacles I had been anticipating, and I figured that if Lori could get past this, then we were home free.

I could see that she was hesitant. I coached her not to look down but to face the mountain at all times, Then I explained that if she would just maintain three points of contact at all times, she would have nothing to fear and would be perfectly safe. It struck me in that moment that maintaining three points of contact in my spiritual life had gotten me safely past the rocky edges in my soul-journey, primarily prayer, fellowship, and God's word. I now negotiated the literal precarious edge before me. When I got to the other side, Lori handed me our hiking poles. After another moment, she began to edge her way across. I stretched toward her, holding onto her backpack as she came across. A moment later she was back on the trail with her feet on solid terra firma. For me the parallel was glaring. In my soul-journey toward inner healing, I had often needed assistance and encouragement from others to get past my own troubled spots in life. Together, Lori and I were now past the worst spot and nearing Trail Crest. My head started to swim, and I felt myself getting dizzy. I paused momentarily as my body adjusted to the change in air pressure. Soon my head was clear again, and we were able to continue up to Trail Crest.

We finally arrived at Trail Crest and were approaching the last leg of our journey. I could just about taste the summit. The icy, cold wind whipped over the top of the mountain. The sky was clear and blue. There wasn't a cloud in sight with the exception of one puffy, little, white cloud in the distance. It was like being in an airplane. I looked down thousands of feet into the valley below us to see what must have been a large lake. The altitude dwarfed the lake, making it look like a small puddle amidst the dark landscape. I knew that the last obstacle would be turning the corner after passing two very large twin spires near Trail Crest. The trail passes behind them creating two windows between them that overlook Lone Pine.

The difficulty in continuing is physical, but also psychological. The mental challenge is accentuated after a person passes by these twin spires. You come around the corner of a rock face and see a very long trail ascending before you leading to the summit. After coming up the arduous Ninety-Seven Switchbacks, many hikers lack the energy and drive to continue when they see the rising trail before them. I thought about how recovery was similar to arriving at Trail Crest. You come to a point when you think you're finally at the top. You start to experience some successes, some healing and wholeness, only to turn a corner and discover that you still have a long way to go. It can be discouraging, and it challenges you both physically and mentally. It's only by God's grace that you can keep making progress. Lori and I were determined to make it to the top. However, you always have to consider that when you make it to the summit of Whitney, you've only gone half the distance. Inevitably, you have to get down the mountain, and that's another 10.7 miles.

We rounded the corner of the twin spires and stopped. The air was thin and our breathing was heavy. I glanced at my watch.

It was nine-thirty. Snow and ice still capped the mountain. Our eyes traced a very thin trail snaking its way up to the summit. Lori balked. Her eyes got wide as she stared at me. I explained to her that all we have to do is get there. Then we could have lunch and rest for an hour. Then it'll be downhill all the way. I must have sounded convincing because we continued up to the summit. We started through a narrow trail packed down with two feet of snow and ice. We were both fatigued continuing only by sheer willpower. An icy crosswind whipped across the snowcap, cutting into our clothing and biting our skin. Elevation sometimes suppresses hunger, but we were both hungry. We kept putting one foot in front of the other, trying to avoid looking at the distance before us. I remembered the moments through my healing where I could only take one step at a time. There were seasons when it was only one day at a time. Progress seemed slow, incremental, tedious, and even arduous at times. I remember wanting to quit and walk away from my mountain of pain and brokenness, but the grace of God pulled me through.

One hour later we were at the summit, finally! Woohoo! What a glorious moment! We made it! I turned slowly around, taking in the grand 360 degree view. It was astounding! It was one of the most incredible experiences of my life! It was a God's-eye view of the world below. I thought about where God had brought me spiritually. It was humbling. God had taken me from the shadowlands below and had walked me through the valley of darkness. He had led me through the tortuous path of healing and deliverance. God had now guided me to the mountaintop both physically and spiritually. Thanks to God, I was now in a place of emotional health unknown to me before, and it was glorious!

Lori and I asked another hiker to take our picture together. There we were. We had reached the summit together, and I knew that it would be a moment we would remember for the rest of our lives. It was absolutely breathtaking! Any detail of the valley below was obscured by our cirrus elevation. Light and dark gray patches of shadowy clouds shrouded the valley thousands of feet below. As I stared down, I could see where we had been and where we were now. I had a new perspective. It was a clear illustration of the spiritual changes made during my ascent from the shadowlands. I would forever see things differently. I now had a God's-eye view of the world and my own destiny. I knew who I was. I understood my spiritual identity, and I could exercise spiritual authority. God had empowered me to conquer my demons and to have victory over my spiritual enemy. I stood there taking it all in. Any problems seemed small and insignificant at this elevation.

As we stood spellbound by the panoramic view, we noticed that the tiny, puffy, cloud that we had seen earlier had become much larger, darker, and more ominous, telegraphing its intention. We sat down between two rocks for shelter from the cold wind, ate lunch, and rested for our journey back down. The day darkened. Fifty-five minutes into our lunch it started to hail. We both looked at each other thinking the same thing. *We need to get out of here!* Unfortunately, life does not allow us to stay on our mountaintops forever. We quickly packed up, threw our backpacks on, and started down the mountain. I looked at my watch. It was 1:05pm.

We made it down near the end of the snow drift in thirty minutes, a lot less time than it took us to come up that same distance. That is when the first thunder clap came like a shock wave. The explosion of sound shook the mountain. It was an awesome demonstration of power at this elevation. We then realized we urgently needed to hurry down. We picked up our pace and were surprised to see other hikers continuing up to the summit as thunder continued to roll over the mountain. As the hail continued to pummel the landscape, we kept our heads down as hail pelted our backs. We could still see our breath in the cold air. We passed the twin spires and headed across Trail Crest. Before we knew it, we were working our way down Ninety-Seven Switchbacks. Angry thunder rocked the heavens above us. The hail turned into rain. The rain fell heavy, pounding us. Runoff came rushing down the center of our trail between our feet. We continued down the switchbacks, moving quickly.

By the time we got down to Trail Camp, the rain was torrential. We still had six more miles to descend and several thousand feet. We started to rock hop to make better time. We started down more switchbacks to Trail Side Meadows, and then stopped suddenly. Our trail was blocked! All the runoff that had been building from the top of the mountain had created a huge waterfall of red mud. Our trail went straight through the falls! The only way down was to plunge our way through. We looked at each other, held our breath, and dived through it head first. We came out the other side only to realize that there were more mudfalls ahead. We were now soaked to the bone. Our rain gear was of no use at this point. We stripped down to t-shirts to stay cool and continued through the next few mudfalls ahead, holding our breath and plunging through each time. These hurdles were unexpected challenges like we often find on our life path. Some of these challenges threaten our progress. Some of these tests may be substantial, some only appear insurmountable. Sometimes we give the enemy more power than he really has, and we are tempted to quit. However, a faith in God, along with determination and commitment, will give us the breakthroughs we need in life, like breaking through cascading mud. The heavy downpour continued throughout the duration of the hike. When we finally passed the signpost for the John Muir Wilderness we were both eager to get back to our camp, shower and get into some dry clothes.

We finally made it back to camp, safe and sound. We were elated and exhausted all at the same time. We showered, ordered a sandwich and fries, eased our way back to our tent, and collapsed on our cots. At first our adrenaline made it hard to sleep, but eventually we were overcome by our need for rest. Now I was in a place of rest not only physically, but also in my spiritual life. God had brought rest and peace into my heart.

Our great adventure was over, and we had reached our goal. In what seemed like a flash, we were soon back home settling into our normal routines once again: working, paying bills, shuttling kids back and forth to school and keeping a schedule. However, on one particular evening when things had slowed down, I took a moment to look around. Here I was in my home where two cute little kids quietly played a video game. I looked over at my beautiful wife who was contentedly reading a book. I marveled at how God had given me a home and a family. I basked in a peace and stability I had never experienced before.

Whitney marked three years of marriage and confirmed to me God's dramatic work in my life. God had restored to me things I could never have recovered on my own. I can truly say with all confidence that I would not be here today without His divine intervention in my life. God enabled me to overcome a huge mountain in my life. He had healed and delivered me and set me free! He had established and blessed me in amazing ways. God had empowered me to reach the summit after bringing me through a very long journey of restoration. He alone had helped me to navigate the shadowlands and come out victorious!

Uncle Jack

NOT LONG AGO, I RECEIVED word that my Uncle Jack passed away. Uncle Jack, the third of my mother's four brothers, had joined the army and served in Special Forces for a period of time. Later, after his time in the service, he traveled the world as a Merchant Marine for a number of years. Uncle Jack was in and out of my life often when I was a boy growing up. Uncle Jack usually came to visit us when his ship was in port. I remember visiting the ports in Long Beach and seeing the name "Buckeye Atlantic" on the side of the very large, dark, rusting freighter that he served on.

It wasn't uncommon for Uncle Jack to give us a surprise visit, bursting through our door with a big grin and a wad of cash, ready to celebrate. He was a good-looking man with dark hair, dark eyes and a strong jaw. Uncle Jack often wore a black turtleneck pullover and was never very frugal with his money, choosing to celebrate on every possible occasion.

Uncle Jack struggled with alcohol, and I remember his demons haunting him for most of his life. Like his dad before him, there was some unseen monster eating away at him. When I was a boy, Uncle Jack took me fishing one day and was pulled over by the police on our way home. I remember my uncle's car being impounded and having to wait at the police station for my dad and mom to come pick me up. He always lived adventurously and was very much a free spirit. He preferred to live life on the edge. That was Uncle Jack.

In the early days when Uncle Jack was in town, he and my parents would go out and celebrate with dinner and drinks at a local place called the Playgirl Club. This establishment was known for giving its patrons a Las Vegas experience. It was during such celebrations and other festivities that Uncle Jack would squander all of his hard-earned cash. It never took long before Jack was depleted financially. Soon he needed to ship out again for a fresh infusion of much needed currency and would catch the next ship out.

We often would not hear from him for a year or so. Once we received news from a relative that Uncle Jack was attacked in a bar and had killed a man in self-defense. Jack ended up serving some time in State Prison for manslaughter. When he was released, he resumed working with the Merchant Marines.

Uncle Jack came and went, and we would see him now and then. Then one day my mother got a phone call from her sister. The phone call was bad news. Uncle Jack had been hitchhiking when the driver who picked him up had a terrible collision with another vehicle. Both of my uncle's legs were badly broken. He was immediately taken to the hospital.

From that day on Jack was no longer able to pass the physical for the Merchant Marines, leaving him landlocked. In the months that followed, Uncle Jack became very depressed and went on a bender. My dad and mom offered to help Uncle Jack get on his feet numerous times, and for a while he would be doing better. Nevertheless, he seemed unable to get decent work. Eventually, discouragement set in, prompting his return to drinking.

Once, I tried my best to talk to Uncle Jack about Jesus. He made it clear to me that he was not interested. Eventually, Uncle Jack applied for disability and started receiving checks. Ironically, it only seemed to make things worse, as he would just drink away what little money he received. Soon he was living on the streets descending further into his addiction to alcohol.

Uncle Jack remained on the streets for many years, sometimes staying in a shelter when the weather was foul. Now and then my mom would put him up for a few days. However, nothing seemed to be able to stop his downward spiral into darkness. He would always be drawn back to drinking, like gravity, like a man possessed by something much stronger than himself. Uncle Jack grew old beyond his years, his hair bleaching white like bones in the desert.

One day my mother received another phone call. It was the call we had all been dreading. Uncle Jack had stopped picking up his SSI checks, something he would never have neglected doing. The phone call was from the Fullerton Police who had found Uncle Jack deceased, lying in the bushes behind a small business, a half empty bottle his only company. He died tormented and alone.

I share Uncle Jack's story because the phone call was a vivid reminder to me that God had saved me from what would have certainly been a similar fate. Jesus' blood had covered the sins that had given evil access into my life. I had walked through the valley of the shadow of death and was not overcome by evil. God's supernatural intervention literally altered the trajectory of my life, my course being changed forever. Jesus Christ shined His light into my life showing me the way out of the shadowlands.

"I will rejoice greatly in the Lord,
my soul will exult in my God;
for He has clothed me with the garments of salvation,
He has wrapped me with the robe of righteousness,
as a bridegroom decks himself with a garland,
and as a bride adorns herself with her jewels."
ISAIAH 61:10 NAS

"... Jesus spoke to them,
saying, 'I am the light of the world:
he that follows Me shall not walk in darkness,
but shall have the light of life."
JOHN 8:12 NAS

Unfortunately, Uncle Jack had been overcome by evil. The Bible warns us to be aware that our enemy, the devil, prowls around like a roaring lion seeking someone to devour. The reality, as I understand it, is that my Uncle had slowly been devoured by a monster bent on destroying his life. This monster had pursued him relentlessly, ultimately causing his death. There is a very real, unseen enemy preying on all of us, plotting our destruction. We are in a battle against spiritual forces we can never overcome without God's help. Uncle Jack had rejected God, leaving him defenseless against the enemy of our souls.

"Be of sober spirit, be on the alert.
Your adversary the devil,
Prowls about like a roaring lion, seeking someone to
devour: But resist him, firm in your faith..."
1 PETER 5:8-9 NAS

If there is one thing that my story illustrates, it's that God is real and available to save, heal, and deliver those who desperately seek Him. God infinitely loves each one of us, but we must seek Him with all our heart, soul, mind, and strength. *"For the eyes of the Lord move to and fro throughout the earth that He might strongly support those whose heart is completely His."* (2 Chronicles 16:9, NAS) I encourage you to seek the Lord, whatever it takes. Jesus Christ, God in the flesh, came to save, heal and deliver all who come to Him. Jesus shed His blood on the cross, died, and was resurrected not only to save us from our sin but to free us from the grip of evil.

God came in the form of Jesus Christ to restore to us what Adam had lost in the Garden of Eden. He came that we might enter our "Promised Land," meaning the fullness of God's favor and blessing. However, we enter that fullness through battle, even as God's word shows the nation of Israel entered their Promised Land through battle. We must learn how to fight this spiritual war to gain our personal victories.

Ultimately, our Promised Land is Heaven, but it is also true that we can enter into God's kingdom blessing on earth right now. Jesus said that the kingdom of God is in your midst, so heaven can be experienced right now! Heaven is experienced through intimacy with God and in loving relationship with those who follow Him. Jesus came so *we might have life and life more abundantly.* (John 10:10) God's very nature delights in healing and restoration. The closer we draw near to Him, the more we receive His restoration and gain more of our full potential.

We were born, and we exist, to walk in God's blessing and to help others enter into the same blessing. However, there is an adversary who strives to keep us from it. Each of us must confront the evil one. This is the adversary that was defeated on the cross, but we must embrace Jesus to appropriate our authority over evil. Moreover, we must learn to exercise our own God-given authority to conquer sin (gain mastery) over it (Genesis 4:7). I had to learn how to do this. I don't know if Uncle Jack ever received Jesus for salvation, but I do know that he never realized God's victory in this life. Uncle Jack, like untold others, was never able to lay hold of it.

There is a battle waging over the hearts and souls of men, women, and children throughout this dark and fallen planet. The dark spiritual forces of this cosmos seek to start wars, divide nations, divide communities, and destroy marriages and families. Ultimately, this evil seeks to destroy each individual by stripping them of any freedom, self-worth or personal sense of value. This spirit of oppression must be defeated in each and every life.

So, at the end of the day, how does a person navigate through this dark, murky, and uncertain world? They do it by seeking, connecting to, and walking with Jesus Christ. In Him are hidden all the treasures of wisdom and knowledge. He is the source of light and life. He is the Wonderful Counselor and the Prince of Peace. He is the Great Physician, our Healer. He is the Everlasting Father. He is our Savior, our Defender, and our Shield. Certainty, truth and illumination are found in Him alone. So, take hold of His hand, for in Him you can successfully *navigate the shadowlands.*

Weapons Training for Spiritual
Warfare and Frontline Ministry
A Guide to Winning Battles In The Spirit Realm

THE PURPOSE FOR *WEAPONS TRAINING for Spiritual Warfare and Frontline Ministry* is to arm the Christian with a working knowledge of how to engage our enemy in battle successfully, taking ground away from the demonic and bringing light into places previously occupied by darkness.

God wants more than anything to see His church (His bride) walk in purity and in victory. This book gives the believer in Christ a working knowledge of the various spiritual weapons made available to them, teaching you how to effectively employ these weapons. This instruction will train you for spiritual battle, so that you might gain the victory in your walk with God and effectively destroy the works of the devil!

You will begin to experience the reality of God's kingdom and dominion over the demonic. Moreover, you will start to become an agent of change in your sphere of influence as God uses you to advance His kingdom. This will bring breakthrough in your life and in the lives of others as you learn *Weapons Training for Spiritual Warfare and Frontline Ministry.*

Contact the author at:

Website: davidallanjacques.com
Email: contact@davidallanjacques.com

Printed in the United States
By Bookmasters